SNOWDONIA TO THE G

A COAST TO COAST WALK ACROSS HIGHEST W

BY JOHN GILLHAM

PHO GR PHS BY JOHN GILLHAM AND VAN GREAVES

British Library Cataloguing in Publication Data

Gillham, John
    Snowdonia to the Gower: a coast to coast
    walk across highest Wales.
    1. Wales. Mountains. Recreation: Walking–Visitors'
    guides
    I. Title
    796.5'22

    ISBN 0-906371-27-9

Front cover photo: Snowdon from the Dog Lakes, Moelwyns
Title page: Tryfan and the Bristly Ridge at sunrise
Contents page: The Carnedd range from the south
Back cover photo: Penard Pill and Three Cliffs Bay, the Gower

ACKNOWLEDGEMENTS I would like to thank those who have helped me in the production of this book. Van Greaves joined the project at an early stage and has made a major contribution to the photographic coverage as detailed study of the credits will reveal. Don Sargeant provided the main route maps and gave me valuable advice for the topographical drawings. Douglas Hughes, Janis Tetlow and Ken Wilson of Diadem Books have given editorial assistance and advice.

    Detailed information about the route has been generously provided by Isobel Thomas (The Gower Society), Cledwyn Fychan (National Library of Wales), Keith Stokes (Welsh Water Authority), David Bown (County Planning Officer, Dyfed) Bob Price and Mrs P. M. Sherwood (Forestry Commission). John Simmons assisted me with the proofreading. I am also indebted to Ken Garrad, Roy, James and Sherril Clayton and Graham Buckley for their companionship on field trips, and to my relatives in South Wales – Albert and Betty Morris and Gwyn and Florence Howells – for their support and hospitality.

    There are over 150 photographs in the book credited as follows [abbreviations – *t* (top), *b* (bottom), *bl* (bottom left) etc]: Van Greaves – rear cover, title page, contents page, 6, 14(2), 15(*b*), 18(*t*), 25(*t*), 28, 32, 33(*b*), 36(*bl* and *br*), 40(*t*), 41, 43, 44(3), 47(2), 48, 50, 53, 54, 58, 61(2), 62, 63(*tr* and *b*), 65, 72(2), 74(*tl* and *tr*), 76(*tr*), 80, 85(2), 86(*t*), 87(*b*), 89, 91, 92, 95(*t*), 97, 98(*b*), 100(*b*), 101(*t*), 102(2), 103(1); Roy Clayton – 25(*b*) and 26; Marion Teal – 60(*t*); Ken Wilson – 77(*bl*), 78(*bl*), 82(*t*), 83(*t*), 84(*t*), 88 and 90; National Library of Wales – 105(*t*) and 108. All other pictures are mine.

JOHN GILLHAM was born in 1947 and grew up in Blackpool although he maintains strong Welsh links through his mother's family – the Emmanuels. He trained as a Quantity Surveyor and currently works as a Supervisor at British Aerospace, Preston. He became interested in mountain walking in 1980 and has since developed a detailed knowledge of the Welsh mountains and the Pennines.

VAN GREAVES was born in Birmingham (1948) where he still lives. After working for the City Council as a Planning Officer he became a professional photographer in 1980 operating first in the commercial field but now increasingly in landscape work. He is an experienced general mountaineer and an accomplished folk singer.

CONTENTS

The Afon Elan at the head of the Elan Valley

INTRODUCTION

Since the inauguration of Tom Stephenson's Pennine Way in 1965 a great number of long distance footpaths have been devised and written about – some official routes having been adopted by local authorities or the Countryside Commission, others purely informal. My route is of the latter category and I would have it no other way, having witnessed the ghastly scars of erosion on the well publicised, waymarked 'Ways'.

Increasing numbers of people have been turning to the fells for recreation, probably in search of peaceful places, far removed from the sprawling urban conurbations that most of us know as 'home', and possibly in response to the challenge that the mountains have always issued. Long distance walking is a natural extension of that challenge – a marathon, a test of endurance. But it is more than that: it takes us to remote, dramatic places where beauty is the norm, gives us the chance to watch the sun go down behind alpine crests, really to taste our camp-cooked food and then sleep under the stars.

I was first persuaded to go fell walking by my nephew who had already been bitten by the bug after a few excursions with his school. His boundless enthusiasm was infectious and I was soon browsing through Ordnance Survey maps planning future expeditions and building mental pictures of mountainscapes from the contour lines. Soon, under my nephew's continued influence, I had graduated to the Pennine Way, but the challenge did not inspire me, although the idea of undertaking a long distance walk did. I do not know if I was inspired by my Welsh ancestry or by childhood memories of camping in Llanrwst, but in September 1981 we both completed a coast to coast walk of Wales – from the Irish Sea to the Bristol Channel. It was a memorable experience and although there were times when the spirits were dulled and dampened by aching limbs and lashing rain, there were those of exhilaration – the feeling of relief when first discarding heavy rucksacks (you feel as if you can run a hundred yards in ten seconds, although I have never tried to prove the point); the camp on Drum in the Carneddau when inverted cloud dissipated leaving visible in a fading sunset the flickering lights of the North Wales coastal towns from Bangor to Prestatyn; and the moments of triumph when inhaling the salt air of Gower and looking out to the sea at journey's end. These are memories that linger!

The trip however illustrated to me the need for a comprehensive guidebook. For the route I had chosen, and which had looked so good on the map, was inadequate in many places, especially when passing through Central Wales. Footpaths had become dilapidated through neglect or were obstructed by barbed wire fences or locked gates. Others crossed ground which was unacceptably boggy or rough. There was little useful literature on anything other than Snowdon and in this light I decided I would research and write my own book.

Having done the route once I knew that a north to south journey through Wales' magnificent land, if the awkward sections were improved, must rank as one of the best walks in Britain. Although 'Offa's Dyke' is such a route it does not reveal the character evident in the more rugged heartlands: the best way would surely be through the mountains.

In planning my route, the objectives were as follows:
1. to find an interesting starting point and memorable terminus on the north and south coasts respectively.
2. to find a safe route intimate to the mountain scenery that is synonymous with Wales, and easily negotiable by the heavily laden mountain camper – it is for him that the walk was primarily designed.
3. to keep the distance short enough to enable an average fell walker to complete the walk within the confines of a two-week holiday.

The small seaside resort of Llanfairfechan, west of Conwy, was a logical starting point, as it lies at the edge of the Carneddau range of mountains which have to be crossed to reach the famous haunts of Snowdonia. There was a choice of points at which to finish the route, but eventually I settled on Three Cliffs Bay on the Gower Peninsular in preference to the equally beautiful Pembrokeshire Coast. There were two reasons for this. Firstly the latter would add an extra day to the journey and secondly the imposing peaks of Carmarthen Fan which precede the Gower would be replaced by seemingly endless perambulations through the lowland farming country that lies west of Llandovery. The finale comprises the tightly enclosed wooded Bishopston Valley which suddenly opens out to reveal the beach at Pwll Du Bay and is followed by a delightful three-mile promenade along the limestone clifftops of Pennard, providing a thoroughly fitting climax to an exciting adventure.

The second of my objectives was harder to satisfy. Some organisations, notably the British Mountaineering Council, believe that long distance foot-

Waterfall, Cwm y llan, Snowdon

with mountain walking in *all* conditions and the other a route which, although intimate with the high mountains, steers a subtle course through, rather than over the ranges. It is worth noting that the latter route still involves more ascent than the Pennine Way! Both routes have their merits, as I think the photographs will illustrate, and it is possible to combine them in various ways to suit the prevailing conditions.

I have often climbed to the summits of the Snowdonian mountains whose towering grey ramparts had, on those early childhood visits, seemed so unyielding and although much of their mystery has been unveiled by my forays, their harsh majesty remains undiminished. Memories of these magnificent peaks are interlaced with those of secluded high tarns lying in the dark quiescence of their ice-sculpted corries.

For all the grandeur of Snowdonia's alpine scenery the moorland peaks and cwms of Central Wales seem to me to be even more appealing. The landscape is simpler in form, but generally it has been less spoiled by man and its remoteness lends a tranquillity seldom equalled. There are countless upland valleys with chattering crystal streams verged by coarse, pale mountain grasses and scattered resilient wind-thrashed rowan trees, which in late summer display vivid scarlet berries. The vast open spaces of this area known as the Elenydd have been divided by monotonous and insensitively planned conifer plantations and decorated with large reservoirs. These additions are not universally popular but few can dispute the fact that the Forestry Commission have provided greatly improved access to the lonely hills and have provided much needed employment and income for the local inhabitants. The Elan Valley reservoirs have had eighty years in which to blend with their environment. This they have done admirably and although the huge stone-built dams contradict the theme they are impressive when the overspill waters thunderously cascade down their walls. Further south, those who pass through Rhandirmwyn on the southern edge of the Elenydd will surely wish to return and explore fully this miniature Snowdonia boasting myriad oaks and many clear trout-filled rivers which meander through steep sided stony hills to reach the verdant pastures of the Tywi Vale.

The entry to South Wales is marked by a return to high mountain country but this time very different in character. Carmarthen Fan (or the Black Mountain) is at the western end of the Brecon Beacon Range and similarly consists of old red sandstone. Glacial action has formed magnificent cliffs on the northern and eastern faces of the group and also provided two lovely tarns Llyn y Fan fawr and Llyn y Fan fach. By comparison the country passed to the north east of Gower is dull but the aesthetic quality is restored on that coastline finale!

And thus we have a personal itinerary for a coast to coast walk – one that can be completed piecemeal or in one go (about a fortnight). Whichever way

paths over high mountain country are unacceptable in that they lead the uninitiated into dangerous terrain, putting unnecessary strain on mountain rescue teams. It therefore seemed sensible to select a route that minimised the time spent on high land, for use by the inexperienced or in times of rough weather. I decided to offer two routes, one mountain route for those familiar

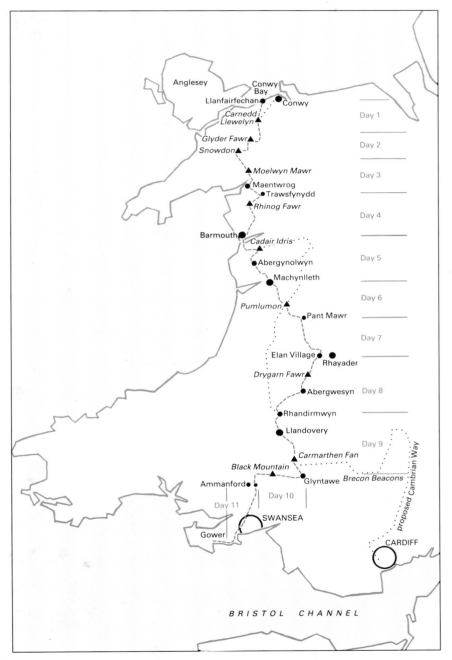

it is undertaken the route will be well remembered for its varied and stimulating scenery. I would like to think that in highlighting lesser-known areas the book will encourage a greater awareness of the beautiful landscapes and interesting places outside Snowdonia. In this the Welsh have surely undersold themselves, choosing instead to invest in the propagation of the already thriving north coast resorts, central Snowdonia and the Pembrokeshire coast.

The authorities should also defend the heritage of the rest of the principality with a little more vehemence for, far too often, spectacular views are marred by unsightly ill-planned developments that would stand no chance of being passed in other National Parks such as the Lake District. Can you imagine the CEGB being allowed to erect a line of electricity pylons in Langdale? Well they have across the Northern Carneddau! There would be a public outcry if Keswick were to become as dilapidated and uncared for as Bethesda (just a few miles from Snowdon!) so why not in Wales?

For all its faults Wales *is* a grand place with a great diversity of scenery. Each mountain range has its own appeal and character – the lofty whaleback ridges of the Carneddau; the bold serrated ramparts of the Glyders; the sheer majesty of Snowdon, truly the monarch of Cambria; the gnarled and faulted flanks of the heather-clad Rhinogs and the wild rolling Elenydd moorlands which rise to their zenith at Pumlumon.

The mountains are divided by many fertile vales sheltering pleasant villages which make good havens for a night's rest. Indeed on such a walk many of the memories of the high fells are enriched by those of convivial evenings at the local pub and the kind and interesting people met. One of the most vivid reminiscences of my first walk across Wales is of being lifted by a superb hot drink at Llandovery's 'Coffee Shop' after being soaked by heavy driving rain which had lasted all morning. I had anticipated with trepidation the crossing of the Carmarthen Fan escarpment but, as I sat staring out of the window, a shaft of sunlight pierced the gloom and someone at the next table commented that the weathermen had forecast sunshine for the next two days. I knew then that I would complete the walk and the discomfort disappeared with the sighting of widening blue skies.

This walk across Wales is therefore a journey of contrasts, of contrasts of scenery and weather, of high windswept moorlands, craggy mountain ridges and idyllic wooded valleys. Of industry, folklore and legend. It provides scope for personal variation according to weather and mood. Wales has a lot to offer those who are willing to explore the landscapes far from the roadsides and what better way to spend a holiday than to don your boots, shoulder your sac and set out on this grand journey from coast to coast through one of the most delightful mountain regions of Britain.

JOHN GILLHAM Blackpool, 1988

*Carnedd Llewelyn and Craig yr Ysfa
seen from the south-east from near
the summit of Pen yr Helgi-Du*

CHAPTER 1

ACROSS THE CARNEDDAU
LLANFAIRFECHAN TO HELYG

The peaks of the Carneddau, the great northern range of the principality are, in the north, smooth-profiled grassy mountains interspersed with the occasional rocky outcrop, but further south, near the Ogwen valley they display rugged cliff-ringed cwms, the Black Ladders (Ysgolion Duon) and Craig yr Ysfa being two of the greatest cliffs in Wales.

Llanfairfechan, a Victorian coastal resort, where our route commences, lies in the shadow of the steely grey scree slopes of Penmaenmawr Mountain, whose form has, over the years, been disfigured by the extensive quarrying activities to provide material for local road building.

The town's intimacy with the mountains makes it an ideal starting point and within half an hour of leaving the stony seashore we are on the rocky crest of Garreg Fawr, gateway to the higher peaks which are spread out to the south. The delights of striding on the lofty ridges of the Carneddau are sampled *en route* to Drum, with expansive views of the Welsh coastline.

The main route and the high-level alternative part company just beyond Drum. On a bright, warm summer's day many walkers will opt to continue along the high route and scale the three-thousand-footers that bar the way to the Ogwen Valley, for these mountains and their high connecting ridges are a joy to walk. In less friendly conditions, however, most will opt to descend to the more sheltered lower route which threads its way through the cwms of Dulyn and Eigiau. These are desolate landscapes. The ruined dwellings are testaments to the plight of those who tried and failed to scrape a living from the infertile soils.

The ascent from Eigiau to Bwlch Trimarchog reveals superb mountain scenery dominated by the cliffs of Craig yr Ysfa on Carnedd Llewelyn's eastern flanks.

On both routes the amiable descent to Ogwen, at the end of a long day, will be remembered for its panoramic views of the peaks of the Glyder group – Tryfan, Glyder Fach and, at the head of the valley, Y Garn.

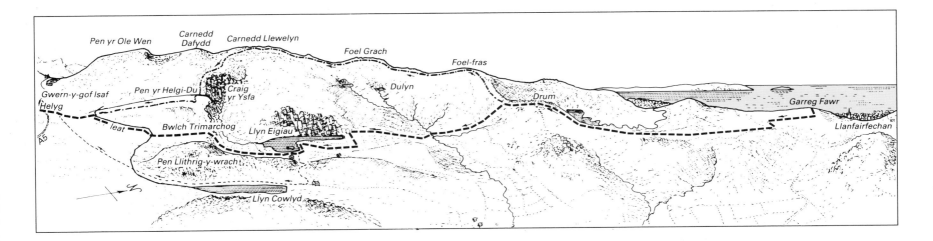

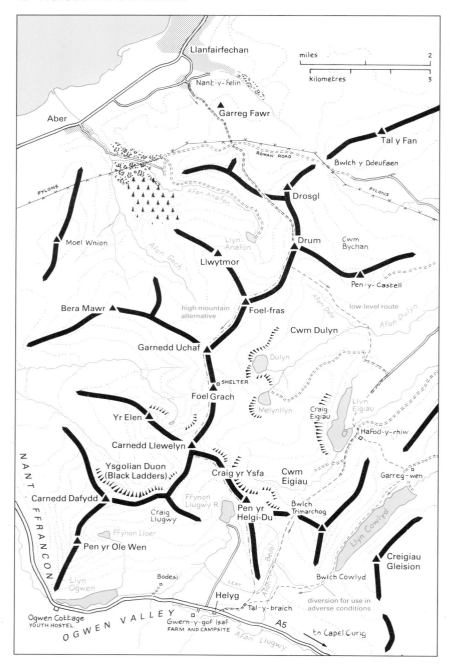

Penmaenmawr Mountain from the shore at Llanfairfechan

There is a temptation on leaving Llan-fairfechan's high street to make a bee-line for the mountains but if one were to take a strictly purist view of a coast to coast walk the starting point would have to be the beach.

A short stroll on the resort's stony shores, inhaling fresh breezes from the Irish Sea, would make a fitting appetizer before heading south up the lane towards Nant-y-felin. The lane twists to the right climbing on the lower slopes of Garreg Fawr which towers above it, obscuring the greater Carneddau peaks which lie not too far behind.

As it levels off, another lane, doub-ling back (east) up the hillside is taken before turning right on a southbound farm track (682739) which takes a steep line up the western flank of Garreg Fawr giving fine views of Llanfairfechan and Anglesey.

Garreg Fawr

On reaching the top of Garreg Fawr, the rocky crest of Tal y Fan, most northerly of Wales's two-thousand-foot moun-tains, comes into view. The southern landscape is badly scarred by rows of unsightly electricity pylons which lead

The pylons at Bwlch y Ddeufaen

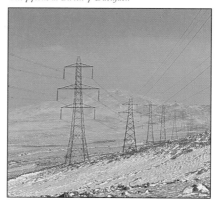

the eye to Bwlch y Ddeufaen, a pass between the peaks of Tal y Fan and Drosgl. A few yards beyond the pylons the path is traversed by an old Roman road leading to Roewen to the east. From Garreg Fawr the route continues along a cart track which ascends the ridge to Drosgl and Drum. The track switches to the western side of the ridge high above the hollow of Llyn Anafon, which sits on a grassy shelf above the river it feeds, dwarfed by the stony fellsides of Llwytmor, Foel-fras and Drum.

In views to the north-west the Afon Anafon meanders gently between the pale hillsides of Llwytmor Bach and Drosgl. It disappears from view by the distant stony slopes of Foel-ganol and the dark conifer forests of Aber.

There is an ethereal quietness on the Northern Carneddau seldom experienced on other Snowdonian hills, and this is particularly evident on the enclosed approaches to Drum. This vast untamed mountain wilderness is now less populated than at any time since the bronze age.

Drum

Drum's summit, where the cart track terminates, is an airy place with good views of the lush Conwy pastures, Llandudno's Great Orme and the Isle of Anglesey, though Foel-fras obscures the Snowdonian giants from view. A circular stone shelter will offer respite from hostile elements.

About 500 yards south of Drum (707692) the ridge is quitted and a steep south-easterly course is taken down grassy slopes following the Afon Ddu to its confluence with the Dulyn. It is accompanied along the whole stretch by a fence which acts as a useful guide in poor conditions.

Cwm Dulyn and Cwm Eigiau

The wide Dulyn Valley is dull and its faded green mantle monotonous. There is little evidence here of the grand mountainscapes that are soon to be unfolded.

The river crossing on a bridge over the Dulyn Intake (where water is conveyed via a tunnel to Llyn Eigiau – see box) precedes a grassy path which rises south-westwards to meet an old farm road. This threads through a strangely contrasting area – overgrown with ferns and thistles. Twisted hawthorn trees grow from bouldered slopes and dilapidated dry stone walls surround small, ruined farm cottages.

A Water Board service road descending from Melynllyn lake is met as the path climbs into Eigiau. First glimpses

The view north from Foel-fras over Llyn Anafon to Conwy Bay

Heading south east in Cwm Eigiau towards Bwlch Trimarchog

The cliffs of Craig yr Ysfa from Cwm Eigiau

Cwm Eigiau and Llyn Eigiau from Bwlch Trimarchog

of the shallow reservoir are seen as the road is followed eastwards to its junction with the terminus of a metalled road. From here a rutted track leading on directly to the Eigiau Dam is followed as far as a stony track at its southern end. This passes below Hafod-y-rhiw, a charming white-walled dwelling in marvellous surroundings. The immense crags of Eigiau rise at the far side of the lake, while the view south-westwards reveals the peaks of Pen yr Helgi-Du and Pen Llithrig-y-wrach, separated by the pass, Bwlch Trimarchog, which is the gateway to the exit from the Carneddau peaks.

Bwlch Trimarchog

The route diverges from the cart track south of the reservoir (719641). Here a

THE DOLGARROG HYDROELECTRIC SCHEME

Those who opt for the low-level route will pass a complex system of leats, pipelines and reservoirs. These belong to the hydroelectric scheme originally devised to supply power to the aluminium works at Dolgarrog, utilising the tremendous energy available from the watercourses that flow from the Carneddau mountains. The scheme involved enlarging Llyn Cowlyd and constructing a new storage reservoir, Llyn Eigiau, but was short-lived as disaster struck soon after its completion.

On the evening of the 3rd November 1925 the powerful pressure of Eigiau's waters burst through the dam, flooding the wide upper valley of the Porth-llwyd before being channelled into the bottleneck of the Dolgarrog Gorge, high above the helpless village. Boulders weighing over two hundred tons were gouged from the mountainsides and thrust down with the raging torrents destroying cottages. A furnace at the aluminium works was flooded resulting in violent explosions.

Sixteen lives were lost that night. It is said that the death toll would have been greater but for the fact that many of the villagers were at the cinema, which is situated on higher ground and was not affected by the floods.

It was discovered, in retrospect, that the dam had been built on insecure ground (moraine debris) and had shifted under the immense pressure of the reservoir's headwater. The dam was never rebuilt and the contracted lake is now some fourteen feet lower than its previous level.

The aluminium works was closed but the power station continues as part of a redesigned scheme and by 1957 four generators were operational for the public supply of electricity.

The present system is served by both high and low-level water catchments. The high-level collects water from the Afon Dulyn and passes it by tunnel to Llyn Cowlyd via Llyn Eigiau. A three mile leat collects the waters of the Ffynnon Llugwy. In the low-level catchment, waters are collected from the Roe, Dulyn, Porth-llwyd and Ddu rivers and fed into the Coedty Reservoir. Pipelines (2 metres diameter reducing to 1.2 metres) convey the water down to the power station from both Coedty and Cowlyd Reservoirs (see sketch).

grassy, reed-lined track leads to the disued farmhouse of Cedryn. A collapsed wall can be followed to Bwlch Trimarchog on an otherwise trackless stretch on rough grassy terrain. Above, on the slopes of Pen Llithrig-y-wrach, are the redundant workings of slate quarries, but the chief point of interest is the gigantic crag Craig yr Ysfa at the head of Cwm Eigiau.

The upper slopes to Bwlch Trimarchog are quite steep but safe except in wintery conditions (see alternative route) but the collar work is rewarded by first glimpses of Moel Siabod which towers above Capel Curig and the wooded hillsides by Nant Gwryd. Snowdon and the Glyder summits are obscured by Pen yr Helgi-Du's southern arm, Y Braich. The retrospective northern views show Craig Eigiau slightly obscuring Llyn Eigiau while in the distance the Conwy Valley meanders to the horizon and the Irish Sea.

The Descent to Ogwen

From Bwlch Trimarchog the descent into the grassy hollow formed by the Afon y Bedol is trackless until the point where the river, a farm road and a leat all converge. At this point trace the left bank of the leat, which veers to the right on the low slopes of Y Braich. Tryfan's shapely profile is revealed as the path nears Tal-y-braich-uchaf. The leat can be crossed by a footbridge at 606700 from where a path descends to the Tal-y-braich farm road which leads down to the A5 at Helyg. Gwern-y-gof Isaf farm, one of the finest mountain camp-sites in North Wales, is situated on the south side of the road 1/3 mile to the east.

Diversion avoiding Bwlch Trimarchog

In very hostile conditions, Bwlch Trimarchog can be avoided by a low, slightly longer, route along the shore of Llyn Cowlyd. From Llyn Eigiau instead

At Bwlch Trimarchog with Pen Llithrig-y-wrach in the background

The leat bridge on the southern slopes of Pen yr Helgi-Du

of passing below Hafod-y-rhiw farm take the road leading to it. The footpath beyond threads through crag-studded, heather slopes before descending to Llyn Cowlyd's barren shore via Garreg-wen farm.

The reservoir is sandwiched between Pen Llithrig-y-wrach's featureless eastern escarpment and Creigiau Gleision, whose rocky-crested ridge commands far more attention despite its inferior height.

The path climbs to Bwlch Cowlyd, where fine views of Ogwen are revealed, and crosses marshy grasslands on a westerly course towards Afon y Bedol and thence south-west to reach the farms of Tal-y-braich, where a lane leads down to the A5 at Helyg.

The view north from Carnedd Llewelyn to Foel Grach

Looking south-east from Carnedd Llewelyn to Pen yr Helgi-Du

THE HIGH MOUNTAIN ALTERNATIVE

Foel-fras

Those who encounter clear weather and decide to stay on the high Carneddau will be rewarded with many grand landscapes on a free-striding ridge walk of epic proportions.

The way from Drum to Foel-fras, the most northerly Welsh three-thousander, is straightforward following either side of the ridge wall. The summit is featureless. A little south of Foel-fras the wall ceases to be useful as it angles sharply towards Cwm Dulyn.

The vast plateaux that lie between here and Carnedd Llewelyn are devoid of distinguishing features and present stiff navigational tests in misty conditions. The north-west slopes gently fall to the wild upper reaches of the Afon Goch valley, guarded on both sides by the ragged crests of Bera Mawr and Llwytmor. On the other side of the ridge the convex slopes prevent views of the lonely mountain tarns of Dulyn and Melynllyn. A cairned path leads to the rock-strewn summit of Garnedd Uchaf, which provides a good viewpoint. The attention is initially drawn to Yr Elen, a well-sculpted, scree-strewn mountain on the western arm of the giant Carnedd Llewelyn. The westerly aspect is focussed along the barren valley of the Afon Caseg which leads down to the town of Bethesda flanked on the south by the Penrhyn Slate Quarries.

Foel Grach

The grassy eminence between Garnedd Uchaf and Carnedd Llewelyn is Foel Grach. An obvious track ascends to this summit, to the north of which lies a mountain refuge hut (usually equipped with first aid supplies), for the use of

The great peaks of Snowdonia seen from Carnedd Llewelyn showing Tryfan (left), the Glyders and Snowdon and the Carnedd ridge leading off right towards Carnedd Dafydd.

travellers caught in extreme conditions.

Carnedd Llewelyn

After a slight depression the climb continues on a broad grassy ridge that rises to the huge flanks of Carnedd Llewelyn, third highest peak in England and Wales and the highest outside the Snowdon group.

The summit, crowned by a couple of shelters and a cairn, is a vast rock-scattered plateau with fine views of most of Snowdonia's principal peaks. The impressive south-western panorama is fronted by Carnedd Dafydd with its sheer northern cliffs – The Black Ladders (Ysgolion Duon). Behind Carnedd

Dafydd is the Glyder range, and beyond this are Yr Wyddfa and Crib-y-ddysgl, Snowdon's two highest tops, looking from here like twins.

The main route traversing the Carneddau continues south-west to Carnedd Dafydd and Pen yr Ole Wen. This would be a feasible way for lightly equipped

walkers and when climatic conditions are good. They would also be rewarded with striking views of Tryfan and the Glyders on their descent down Pen yr Ole Wen's East Ridge (avoid the tortuous screes of the south side) to the eastern end of Llyn Ogwen but this descent is steep and arduous, coming at the end of

Craig yr Ysfa from the summit of Pen yr Helgi-Du

Descending to Helyg from below the leat bridge with Tryfan in the background

the day and probably best avoided by those with heavy rucksacks. A half-way alternative takes the amicable slopes leading down to the Ogwen Valley at Bodesi from Craig Lugwy.

Craig yr Ysfa

Probably the best way on from Carnedd Llewellyn is to descend the east–south-east ridge to the cliffs of Craig yr Ysfa with its sudden dramatic view down a huge gorge known as The Amphi-theatre. This is flanked on the left by sheer cliffs and on the right by the pin-nacled ridge of Amphitheatre Buttress. A wide scree fan sweeps out of The Amphitheatre to the head of Cwm Eigiau more than a thousand feet below. The Amphitheatre is untypically rocky –

as from the ridge the cliffs appear for the most part heavily vegetated though very steep.

The path continues down above the cliff in a series of tricky rock steps where extra care must be exercised especially in wet or icy conditions. However, these intricacies are short-lived and the col between Craig yr Ysfa and Pen yr Helgi-Du is reached. From here you may see walkers toiling up the steep shaly path from the shores of the Ffynnon Llugwy Reservoir, which is now reached by a Water Board road and offers a quick but dull descent to Helyg.

It is much more pleasurable to take the short steep ascent to Pen yr Helgi-Du by a steep path that threads between crags interspersed with bilberry and heather. Although a steadying hand is occasionally needed on this ascent, nowhere could the way be classified as hazardous. A path that traverses the mountain's western slopes marks the start of the steepest section and here is a good place to enjoy the scene across Ffynnon Llugwy towards Tryfan, whose profile from this viewpoint is wedge-like and stands proud of the loftier Glyders.

Pen yr Helgi-Du's summit is the culmination of a grassy whale-back ridge, Y Braich, which ends abruptly, its northern craggy slopes sweeping to the depths of Cwm Eigiau. At their foot lies an old quarry with the course of its tramway still discernible, a reminder of a bygone industry. How different must this now remote valley have seemed when the noises of man and machinery filled the air.

The descent is an easy one, following the gentle grassy spur of Y Braich to join the Bwlch Trimarchog route at the leat. Go through the gate, cross the bridge over the leat and descend to the A5 at Helyg and thence to Gwern-y-gof Isaf.

CHAPTER 2

THE GLYDERS AND SNOWDON
HELYG TO NANTGWYNANT

Is a walk through High Wales complete without scaling its loftiest peak, Snowdon?

For experienced backpackers looking for a high mountain challenge walk across the principality, the answer has to be no: Snowdon and the Glyders are a 'must'. I must stress however, that as backpacking routes, they are arduous; only the fittest could safely complete both ranges within one day and clear conditions would be advisable.

Those who are already familiar with these mountains may well be searching for new scenery and our main route should fit the bill. The ascent to the Glyder ridge via Braich y Ddeugwm has often been written of in glowing terms, but I have seldom seen anybody use this route, from which the finest views of Tryfan's buttresses may be enjoyed. The way down to Pen-y-Gwryd and thence along the lonely, unspoiled Siabod-Moelwyn ridge is rewarded by views of the Snowdon group, slowly and subtly changing, which capture the attention throughout. The final section of the route is characterised by endless permutations of intricate bluffs, secluded tarns and reedy shallow pools, many unrecorded on the maps; a ridge with countless quiet corners that are ideal natural mountain campsites. My favourites are near the tarn on the summit of Y Cribau and by the south-western lake of the Llynnau'r Cwn (Dog Lake) trio (662486).

For convenience of staging I have included descents to Nantgwynant. Although hard won ascent is lost, it may be necessary to replenish supplies at the post office/general store, or inclement weather may make it expedient temporarily to abandon the high ground. The ridge walk connection between Llyn Edno (the exit point to Nantgwynant) and Llyn yr Adar (where the low-level campers and those who have followed the high mountain route regain the ridge) is included for the discriminating backpackers who decide to make camp in this high paradise.

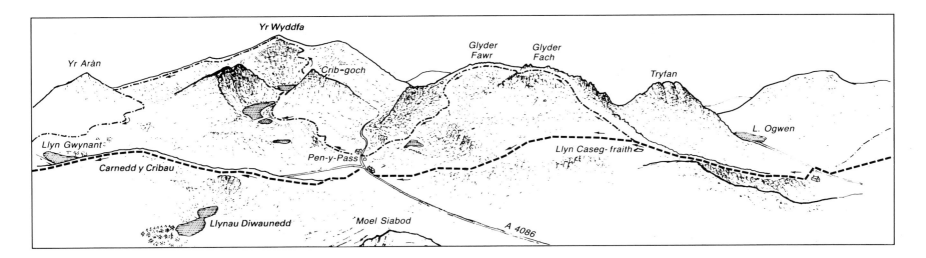

Ascending Braich y Ddeugwm past Tryfan to gain the Glyder ridge near Llyn Caseg-fraith (inset)

Braich y Ddeugwm

Our route to the Glyder ridge begins at Gwern-y-gof Isaf (685602) and rises on a spur, Braich y Ddeugwm, which is only named on OS 1:25,000 maps.

The best course is to keep to the crest of the spur except for the initial stretch, where a stile on its western side straddles an electric fence. The steep, grassy path rises amongst crags and affords truly memorable views of Tryfan across its wild and little-frequented cwm. The gradient eases as Llyn Caseg-fraith is reached. A sketchy track passes through the marshy surrounds to the north of the lake and its tiny attendant pools. After rising to the head of Cwm Tryfan it meets the Miners' Track that links Ogwen and Pen-y-Gwryd. From here Glyder Fach's jagged northern spur, aptly named Bristly Ridge, vies for attention with Tryfan's magnificently sculpted buttresses in a view which also encompasses the Carneddau peaks.

The Descent from the Glyder Ridge

The Miners' Track crosses a grassy plateau before descending the craggy upper southern slopes of Glyder Fach. The Nant Ddu (stream) is passed beneath a fine cascade. Much of the rock is replaced by heather, whose vivid purple summer mantle makes a brilliant foreground to the wide southern vista which includes Moel Siabod, Cnicht and the Moelwyns separated from the Snowdon Group by the curving Gwynant valley. In one of Snowdon's finest facades Crib-goch, Yr Wyddfa, and Crib-y-ddysgl appear huddled, all displaying classical mountain form. Reddish hues that give rise to the name, Crib-goch (red ridge) can be seen on the cliffs that tumble to the Pass of Llanberis. Beyond the hidden hollow of Cwm Dyli lie the twin summits of Lliwedd linked to the range's principal peak by a precipitous ridge.

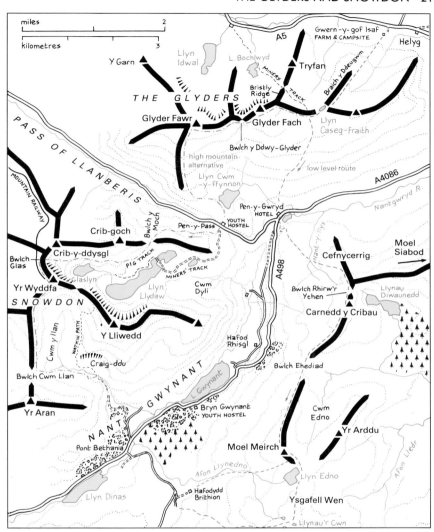

Pen-y-Gwryd

As it nears the valley floor, the Miners' Track crosses a dry stone wall which it follows to the Nantgwryd river and thence across an undulating field to meet the road just east of the Pen-y-Gwryd Inn. The PYG, as the inn is affectionately known, has for a century been a promi- nent centre for the exploration of the Welsh Mountains, as well as the plan- ning of Himalayan and Alpine expedi- tions. Here John Hunt (now Lord Hunt) and his team, who in 1953 were the first to climb Everest, met to make the final preparations before departing for Nepal. On their re-union at the PYG they pre-

The Pen-y-Gwryd Hotel

sented landlord and fellow climber Chris Briggs with a piece of summit rock which is still kept here. The 'Climbers' Bar' has a ceiling which has been autographed by many climbers including the summit pair, Sir Edmund Hillary and Sherpa Tenzing. The inn offers good food including excellent quiches, salads and apple pie, and makes an ideal lunch stop.

Cefnycerrig

Beyond the PYG the route once more ascends, this time to the Siabod/Moelwyn ridge. A second stile on the eastern side of the Beddgelert road (A498) allows entry to the marshy land north-west of Cefnycerrig, the rock-crested spur rising to the main ridge. Traverse the northern slopes of the small hill ahead and make a bee-line (south-east) for Cefnycerrig's lowest crags crossing the Nant-y-llys on the way. The track, marshy in places, then follows a fence to the ridge at Bwlch Rhiw'r Ychen (676540 – not marked on 1:50,000 maps). Both

sides of the pass are guarded by vegetated crags which overlook Llynau Diwaunedd, remotely situated beneath Moel Siabod's barren, featureless south-facing slopes. Forestry Commission conifer plantations now surround three sides of the tarn. I can only hope the Commission's lust for new lands in the Snowdonia National Park will be vigorously resisted as further intrusions could seriously detract from the aesthetic appeal of this mountain scenery.

Carnedd y Cribau

From the bwlch, a path bordered by the ridge-fence twists amongst bilberry and boulders on a steep but short pull to the airy summit of Carnedd y Cribau. The succeeding ridge is punctuated by a series of delightful shallow tarns which provide interesting preliminaries to the last steep fall to Bwlch Ehediad, a dull, grassy hollow preceding the rise to Moel Meirch. (NB Youth Hostellers bound for Bryn Gwynant should leave the ridge here using a path heading north-west.)

Moel Meirch

A narrow track ascends alongside the fence, hereabouts dilapidated, and heads towards the rocky crest of Moel Meirch. It passes through intricately-faulted and gnarled rock formations interspersed with deep heather. Just north of the summit are two boggy areas which can be avoided by keeping to the west side on heathered verges. A visit to Moel Meirch's very highest point will necessitate a slight detour and a short scramble westwards from the path at the head of Cwm Edno.

Llyn Edno

Llyn Edno's appearance is sudden. It will have been anticipated for quite a while but frequent rocky knolls have marred all previews. The trout-filled lake occupies a shallow stony basin south of Moel Meirch and is a favoured spot for anglers. Looking westwards

beyond Llyn Edno, the view of Snowdon highlights the profile of that knife-edged ridge between Crib-y-ddysgl and Crib-goch, whose pinnacles are plainly visible. To their left is the pointed summit of Yr Wyddfa which dwarfs the Lliwedd peaks which are seen end on.

Descent to Nantgwynant

Walkers who have rejected the idea of a high-level camp can quit the ridge by following the Afon Llyn Edno as it descends to the Nanmor Lane. The river is very beautiful in its lower course where it bounds vigorously amongst rocky slopes lined with colourful rhododendron bushes. The path meets the lane beyond Hafodydd Brithion farm (640494) just one mile short of Nantgwynant.

Ridge route via Ysgafell Wen and Llyn yr Adar

I have to recommend that in calm con-

Moel Siabod and Llynau Diwaunedd from Carnedd y Cribau

The view east to Snowdon and the Glyders from Llynnau'r Cwn, near the summit of Ysgafell Wen

ditions a mountain camp be made. On this section of the ridge there are numerous secluded and sheltered sites where one can relax and watch the sun set behind the peaks of Snowdon. The path rises south-east from Llyn Edno to Ysgafell Wen whose steep eastern brow overlooks the marshlands that are the source of the Afon Lledr. The heather of Moel Meirch has been replaced by more verdant hill pastures although the frequent rock outcrops remain.

A small reedy tarn, the most easterly of Llynnau'r Cwn (The Dog Lakes) is seen from the highest point of the ridge. A trackless south-westerly course from the eastern tarn will descend to Llyn yr Adar, another anglers' retreat, though they have competition from the hundreds of gulls who flock to the islet at the centre of the lake. The views of Snowdon from here are superior to those from Llyn Edno for the ridge obscures less of its lower slopes: much of the Watkin Path can be traced.

Llyn yr Adar is not an ideal place for camping although the views are terrific. It is too exposed and its shores are a little too marshy for tents. The area around the Dog Lakes is much better.

On the north-eastern shores of Llyn yr Adar the path converges with the one that has ascended from Nantgwynant via Llyn Llagi (described in the next chapter).

The fine view of the Snowdon horseshoe from the southern slopes of Glyder Fawr on the (waymarked) descent to Pen-y-Pass

THE HIGH MOUNTAIN ALTERNATIVE

Glyder Fach

From the head of Cwm Tryfan (667583) the high mountain route takes a westerly direction on an increasingly rocky path to Glyder Fach's summit. Always prominent in the view ahead is the narrow jagged spur of Bristly Ridge descending steeply to Bwlch Tryfan.

Glyder Fach's bouldery summit plateau has noteworthy (and much photographed) features which include 'The Cantilever' a large, flat slab securely supported at one end by a group of vertical pillars, and 'Castle of the Winds' (Castell y Gwynt), a huge, serrated outcrop obstructing the way to Glyder Fawr beyond. The descent of Glyder Fach involves skirting around the southern side of the castle to gain Bwlch y Ddwy-Glyder situated high above Llyn Bochlwyd.

Glyder Fawr

The way to Glyder Fawr is now gradual and easy going but confusing in misty conditions. In clear weather the views are magnificent. To the north, beyond the Nameless Cwm and Llyn Idwal, the gaze can wander to the rugged Pen yr Ole Wen and down the Nant Ffrancon to the Menai Straits and the flat plains of Anglesey. However, it is the great Snowdon massif to the south-west that commands most attention. The four peaks that surround the great glaciated hollow of Cwm Dyli form a distinctive skyline in which the classic Snowdon Horseshoe walk can easily be traced.

Glyder Fawr's extensive top is not so rough as its smaller neighbour but is made interesting by frequent teeth-like rock protruberances.

The descent south from the summit is waymarked by red arrows painted on rocks assisting route-finding to Pen-y-Pass and leading walkers away from the complex cliffs of Llanberis Pass. Although intended to help with navigation, they have invoked considerable ire in some mountaineering circles. In my opinion these markings are fairly unobtrusive and a positive aid, in misty conditions, to a safe descent, though one wouldn't wish them to proliferate elsewhere.

In its lower reaches the path meanders through a more grassy terrain, although there is no shortage of boulders on which to daub the red arrows. As Yr

The view from Glyder Fach to Llyn Caseg-fraith and Moel Siabod

Pen-y-Pass from the Pig Track near Bwlch y Moch

Crib-goch and Cwm Dyli seen from the ridge between Bwlch Glas and Snowdon's summit

Wyddfa sinks from view behind their ridge Crib-y-ddysgl and Crib-goch assume greater prominence in the scene across the valley. Llyn Cwm-y-ffynnon, a squarish-shaped lake in a shallow marshy hollow, is passed via its south-western shore before the short, steep descent to the Pen-y-Pass Youth Hostel which stands at the head of the wild Pass of Llanberis.

Pen-y-Pass

Across the road is the Gorphwysfa Restaurant which is an ideal place to rest and dine before tackling Snowdon. (NB At least four and a half hours will be needed to complete the section to Nantgwynant.)

There are two alternative direct routes to Snowdon from here – the Miners' Track and the Pig (frequently misnamed

PYG) Track. The former is a good path that skirts the lakes of Teyrn, Llydaw and Glaslyn in the cradle of Cwm Dyli before climbing the zig-zags to Bwlch Glas and thence to the summit. This popular track passes close to the derelict copper mines. The Pig Track climbs westwards out of the Llanberis Pass to Bwlch y Moch (Pass of the Pigs) before entering Cwm Dyli. Its course fits more naturally with its mountain surroundings with a greater variety of views and is thus chosen as the primary route.

increasingly vie for attention.

Bwlch y Moch

Bwlch y Moch provides a natural stopping place to savour the grandeur of the scene around Cwm Dyli, where the expansive, blue-green waters of Llyn Llydaw lie far below. The Miners' Track can be seen crossing the lake via a causeway that can be submerged after prolonged periods of rain. Beyond Llyn Llydaw vertical cliffs rise to the twin summits of Y Lliwedd. Yr Wyddfa at the head of the cwm is visible over the

Y Lliwedd and Y Gribin seen across Glaslyn from the Pig Track

---

AFANC

Afanc was a fearsome monster who dwelt in Llyn-y-afanc, a deep pool on the Afon Conwy near Betws-y-Coed. When the mood took him he would use his mysterious powers to cause flooding to the surrounding areas, creating havoc and hardship for the local inhabitants. After a particularly bad flood these men were hell-bent on ridding themselves of this creature and devised a plan.

Now Afanc was known, as many vile beasts are, to be easy prey for the ladies,

and so he was lured out of his pool by the most beautiful damsel they could muster. As the monster appeared he was set upon and bound in chains by many men, who had been hiding in the nearby bushes. The chains were then attached to two giant oxen who dragged Afanc across the shoulder of Moel Siabod down to Gwynant and then on to Cwm Dyli, where, in the deep waters of Glaslyn, he was dumped. Some say he lives there still.

THE LEGEND OF KING ARTHUR'S DEMISE

Sir Modred, a treacherous knight formed an alliance with the Saxons to overthrow the ageing King Arthur. Their armies congregated in the hills of Snowdonia. Arthur discovered the plan and marched to confront the rebels; they met at Tregalan above Cwm y llan. The battle that ensued was a bloody one but slowly Arthur forced his enemy up the hillside to the pass between Yr Wyddfa and Y Lliwedd.

In the murky winter dusk Arthur was

hit by an arrow, but before dying it is said that he slew Sir Modred with a flash of his mighty sword, Excalibur. The place of their deaths has since been known as Bwlch-ysaethau, Pass of the Arrows.

Sir Bedivere carried the King down to Llyn Llydaw where he was ferried away. The few remaining knights withdrew to a hidden cave in Lliwedd's precipices waiting for their leader to re-emerge. The legend has it that they still wait . . .

A signpost guides the walker to the path which scales the northern slopes of the hill known as the 'Last Nail in the Horseshoe'. Crib-goch is always prominent, towering above the Llanberis Pass. Glyder Fawr's south-western crags, particularly the last outlier, Esgair Felen,

shoulder of Crib-goch, where the path divides. One way ascends directly to Crib-goch and the other, which is the Pig Track, traverses its southern slopes.

Cwm Dyli

As the well-trodden path rises gradually across Crib-goch's slopes it provides a

viewpoint from which it is possible to see, high above on the northern skyline, climbers tentatively scaling the pinnacles of Crib-goch.

After about a mile a spur is crossed and Glaslyn is revealed beyond. The path veers north-north-west above the outfall of the deep green lake which is tightly encircled by the precipitous dark cliffs and screes of Yr Wyddfa and Crib-y-ddysgl. The lake was once believed to have been bottomless and is the subject of a legend involving a damsel and a monster. The nearby cliffs of Y Lliwedd and Bwlchysaethau are also linked to legend (see box). The Miners' Track climbs from the shores of the lake to meet our route which now begins its spectacular ascent out of Cwm Dyli via the 'zig-zags'. (If time is pressing the route can be shortened at this point by taking the Y Gribin ridge that links the eastern end of Glaslyn with Bwlchysaethau. This is a stiff scramble, comparable to Crib-goch or the Bristly Ridge, but it does allow the Watkin Path to be reached with-

out an arduous climb over Yr Wyddfa).

The section of the path that leads up to the crest of the ridge above has been so scarred and eroded by storms and walkers that it has attracted the attention of the path 'improvers'. A painted metal sign, which would not look out of place in a Manchester subway, directs the walker along a blatantly obvious rock-slabbed stairway that gains the height in one large 'zig', thus avoiding the previous eroded slopes. This unnatural intrusion into such a wild scene is jarring and will probably take many years to blend acceptably with its surroundings.

Bwlch Glas

A huge monolith marks the exit of the track at Bwlch Glas, the pass between Snowdon's two highest summits. This makes a junction with the long walking route from Llanberis and the Snowdon Mountain Railway. There now remains a short easy ascent following the line of crags at Cwm Dyli's edge. This route is preferable to the parallel railway track as the vistas of Cwm Dyli are seen at their

Looking north from the summit of Snowdon showing the final section of the mountain railway

best from the ridge half-way between the bwlch and Yr Wyddfa's summit. From here Llyn Llydaw and Glaslyn can be seen in their entirety surrounded by the ridges of Lliwedd, Crib-y-ddysgl and Crib-goch which together with Yr Wyddfa comprise the 'Snowdon Horseshoe'. The razor-like edge of Crib-goch's pinnacles can be appreciated standing out boldly in front of the more distant panorama of the Glyders and Moel Siabod.

Yr Wyddfa

The flat-roofed monstrosity of Snowdon's 'hotel' and railway terminus is hated by all when closed and used by most when open. I for one do not begrudge the king's ransom demanded at the bar for a can of lager when I have toiled long on a hot summer's day.

For all its commerciality the summit of Snowdon offers the finest vistas in all Wales. To the west beyond the Nant y Betws and Llyn Cwellyn is Mynydd Mawr where smooth grassy slopes ter-minate abruptly at the shattered Craig y bera whose broken crags disintegrate into immense screes. In the foreground the dark cliffs of Llechog command a cwm housing three shallow tarns. The view northwards is dominated by the railway gradually descending the grassy escarpment to Llanberis. In the southern panorama, Cnicht and the Moelwyns lead the eye to the more distant and hazy mountains of the Harlech Dome and Cadair Idris.

The South Ridge and Cwm y llan

A narrow ridge declining south-west to Bwlch Main and thence southwards is used on the descent from Snowdon's summit.

This descent is dramatised by views to the left where the severe cliffs of Clogwyn Du plunge over 2,000ft to Cwm y llan, a gigantic hollow enclosed by the stony flanks of Lliwedd and Yr Aran to the south. At the cwm's verdant base lie the ruins of the South Snowdon Slate Works.

After a slight ascent to a subsidiary top known as The Saddle, the route heads towards Bwlch Cwm Llan (605523) (not marked on 1:50,000 maps).

At the bwlch, distinguished by a small tarn and quarry, the route descends eastwards on Yr Aran's grassy slopes to join the firm track of a dismantled tramway, south of the great cliff of Craig-ddu. It meets the popular Watkin Path near to the stone ruins of Plas Cwm Llan. I have often seen tents pitched here and it looks a good site, being next to the river.

Nantgwynant

As the arms of Lliwedd and Yr Aran close around the brim of the cwm, the river vigorously comes to life thundering down in a series of cataracts and a very impressive waterfall to the plains of Nantgwynant.

The barren mountainsides now wear a new verdant mantle. 'Real' trees, not the blanket of tedious Forestry Commission conifer plantations, but small natural copses, which line the slopes accentuating their majestic form. The path that winds into Nantgwynant is a solidly constructed one, and as 'im-proved' paths go is reasonably tasteful. The view of the mountains to the south are to the craggy Moelwyn range and Cnicht, with its well-spaced twin summit bluffs.

After passing the pleasant Parc Hafod-y-llan woods, which are lined with rhododendron, a lane leads to the Beddgelert-Capel Curig road at Pont Bethania.

For those who are to stay the night in the valley there is a campsite at Llyndy-isaf farm (626498); the Bryn Gwynant Youth Hostel is one mile away on the Capel Curig road, and the hotels of Beddgelert are a little less than four miles south-west. (This is best reached by a beautiful walk south of Llyn Dinas and the Afon Glaslyn.) Those preferring a mountain camp might well press on to Llyn Llagi (650483) a beautiful tarn situated beneath huge dark cliffs that rise to the Moelwyn ridge.

A camp above Llyn Gwynant looking south-west to Moel Hebog and Yr Aran

The Cwm Llan waterfalls below the Watkin Path with the Snowdon massif in the background obscured by low cloud

CHAPTER 3

THE MOELWYNS
NANTGWYNANT TO TRAWSFYNYDD

Those who camped on high will, with a little luck, be blessed with clear morning sunlight embellishing the crags and cwms of Snowdon and glinting on the waters of a Moelwyn tarn. They will eat their bacon and eggs with the comforting knowledge that most of the day's toils have been avoided by not making the descent to Nantgwynant on the previous afternoon.

Provided that they were not over-indulgent at a Beddgelert alehouse, those who did make that descent will enjoy superb scenery to recompense the extra effort involved in the reascent of the Moelwyn ridge. Especially memorable are the retrospective views of Snowdon and the dark broken cliffs that tower above the high and lonely tarn, Llyn Llagi.

The northern Moelwyn ridge is unspoilt but there is stark contrast at Bwlch y Rhosydd to the east of Cnicht. Here, at the derelict Rhosydd Quarries, the mountainsides have been cut and scarred revealing their blue Ordovician core, but for all their ugliness, the ravages and relics of these old workings arouse immense interest and curiosity in the traveller. There is a strange silence about the place and yet the reverberations from bustling activities of its past are ever-present in the imagination.

The quarries are overlooked by the airy summits of Moelwyn Mawr and Moelwyn Bach, little frequented by Snowdonian standards but with their strategic position at the heart of the National Park offering walkers extensive vistas of neighbouring peaks as well as the incongruous Stwlan Dam.

The gentle verdant scenery in the sheltered oak woods of Coed Maentwrog and the lush pastures of the Vale of Ffestiniog form a pleasant contrast to the quarry-scarred Moelwyns. The picturesque village of Maentwrog, hiding in a quiet corner away from the busy A487 highway, is another point of interest.

The first taste of the rugged Rhinog scenery is sampled west of Llyn Trawsfynydd where the range's last rampart, Moel y Gyrafolen declines to its shores. The lake shore is also 'graced' by the infamous Trawsfynydd Power Station set unnervingly close to the village that provides a strategic end to the day's efforts.

Nantgwynant

A narrow, winding lane leaves the A498 at Nantgwynant (626503) and rises in a general south-easterly direction towards the Moelwyn ridge. Opposite the converted chapel of Blaen Nant (635490), a path heads east, descending to cross a small stream with a farm building on the right. Delightfully situated amongst oak and rhododendron, the white-washed farmhouse, Llwynyrhwch, is passed to the north. From here a well-defined track winds through a complex but beautiful landscape of pasture, dry-stone walls, foaming cataracts and busy streams flowing through broad-leafed

Llyn Llagi from the north east

copses: and always standing proud in the view ahead – the broken, heather-clad crags of Ysgafell Wen and Moel Meirch.

The land is more marshy as the path approaches Llyn Llagi, a circular tarn completely overshadowed by the sombre vertical cliffs that tower from its eastern edge. The expanse of rock is briefly interrupted by a cascade which is fed by the waters of Llyn yr Adar six hundred feet above.

Llyn yr Adar

A well-cairned track rises eastwards to avoid the precipices. Just beyond a stream crossing, at a point marked by a large cairn, the track turns to the south

A retrospective view to the Snowdon group from the Moelwyn range east of Llyn yr Adar

rising on a bouldery course to the ridge before veering south-west to reach the shores of Llyn yr Adar. This is circumvented on its east side through marshy grassland to the col between Ysgafell Wen and Cnicht (657477). This latter peak is famous when viewed from the south-west from where it is seen as a Matterhorn in miniature. Its profile is less arresting from the east but it can easily be climbed. A well worn south-west bound path leads to the summit, a worthwhile diversion for strong walkers who will be able to make up the extra hour required. Their efforts will be rewarded with wide panoramas across Tremadog Bay and the Rhinogs, unrestricted views of Snowdon's southern face and an interesting angle on Moelwyn Mawr, which displays the scars of defunct quarrying activities.

The main route, however, descends south-eastwards in a series of rocky shelves at the head of Cwm-y-foel, whose shapely lake beneath the screes of Cnicht lies precariously close to the edge of the cavernous Cwm Croesor.

Bwlch y Rhosydd
After passing the small reservoir of Cwm-corsiog the path descends further to Bwlch y Rhosydd, a high pass between Cwm Croesor and Cwmorthin.

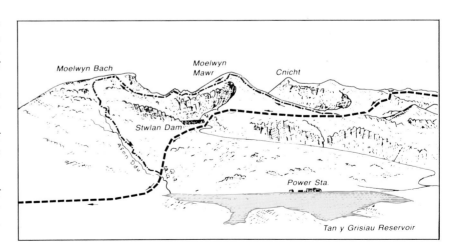

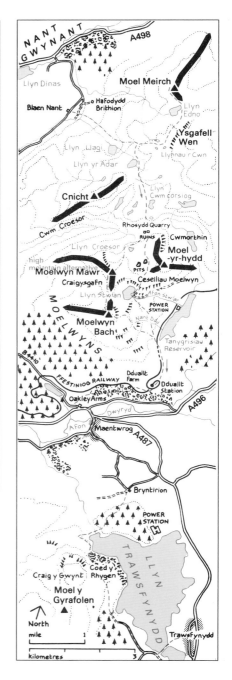

Relics of slate workers' houses in lower Cwmorthin

Here, just sixty years after the closure of the huge slate quarries and mines, the buildings lie dilapidated, crumbling into the surrounding slag heaps. The blue-grey scars slowly heal beneath mossy and lichenous scabs as the quarry is slowly masked by nature.

Behind the quarry buildings, colossal spoil heaps litter the swelling slopes of Moel-yr-hydd and Moelwyn Mawr whose grassy apexes just rise above the ravages of industry. In a peaty hollow between the peaks, amongst further slate workings, lie two cavernous collapsed mine chambers.

The industrial relics have their uses however and an old tramway behind the main quarry building provides a route out of Bwlch y Rhosydd (not marked on 1:50,000). The path passes east of one of the spoil heaps and quarry pits before reaching the depression between Moel-yr-hydd and Moelwyn Mawr. At just over 1,800ft this is the highest point of the main route in the southern Moelwyns and from here a descent must be made to the Vale of Ffestiniog. The descent commences in a southerly direction across splintered slaggy slopes followed by a wet grassy course above the cliffs of

Ceseiliau Moelwyn.

Llyn Stwlan

At the cliff's edge we are confronted by the Stwlan Reservoir, man's most savage affront to the Moelwyn's dignity. This reservoir and the larger Tanygrisiau Reservoir, seen still further down the eastern mountainside, are part of the Ffestiniog Power Station and Pumped Storage Scheme (see box). The concrete monstrosities of dam and intake gates are totally alien to an otherwise magnificent scene.

From the sterile lake-shores rises the majestic slope of Moelwyn. Moelwyn Bach at its far side is characterised by a profile that resembles a human face. The quartz-veined rock facade of the ridge, Craigysgafn rises to its zenith at the domed summit of Moelwyn Mawr.

The descent to Llyn Stwlan skirts the precipitous crags on its north-west shore and care must be exercised as there are one or two tricky parts.

A tarmac lane is encountered at the northern end of the dam and this is used

FFESTINIOG POWER STATION AND PUMPED STORAGE SCHEME

The Stwlan Dam from Craig Ysgafn

The scheme, completed in 1963, was designed as a low cost answer to two problems. Firstly, there was a need to utilise surplus power generated by the large modern stations (especially nuclear ones) which needed to be run continuously to be efficient. Secondly, there was a requirement to supply extra electricity to cope with peak demands.

Pump storage units need two reservoirs at different levels. The existing Llyn Stwlan, high in the Moelwyns, was enlarged and a new reservoir at Tanygrisiau was created by damming the Nant Ystradau and flooding its natural basin. The Power Station building, two thirds underground, was constructed next to the lower reservoir.

At night, when electricity requirements are low, the surplus power is used to pump water from the lower to the upper reservoirs. When electricity is needed the intake gates are opened and water is released down tunnels at high pressure to power the turbines. In this way 360 megawatts can be generated in less than a minute.

Moelwyn Mawr from slate heaps in upper Cwmorthin

until it reaches the Afon Stwlan at the dam's other edge. After crossing the stream a path leads south-eastwards to the huge Tanygrisiau reservoir.

Tanygrisiau and Coed Maentwrog

For much of the way the path traces the course of an old stone wall. It then meets the Nant Ddu, a lively stream which is crossed using a footbridge set amongst trees and a ruin. From here continue to the southern tip of the lake beyond which the Ffestiniog narrow gauge railway is crossed. An unsurfaced lane leads southwards joining the old course of the railway (now dismantled) north of Dduallt Station, whose platform constitutes part of the route.

The path crosses the railway track just south of the station and heads southwest across grassy slopes before descending to and recrossing the line to the east of Dduallt farm. The way continues down through a splendid oak wood – Coed Maentwrog, now a designated nature reserve, and emerges above the lovely Vale of Ffestiniog where the Afon Dwyryd lazily meanders through its wide, green-pastured valley.

Maentwrog

On leaving the oakwoods the path meets the B4410 near to the Oakley Arms (659409). The charming village of Maentwrog is reached by following this road past the hotel, turning left along the A487 and then crossing the old three-arched bridge, which carries the A496

The Afon Dwyryd at Maentwrog

A view across Llyn Trawsfynydd to Moelwyn Bach with the Snowdon group beyond

over the Afon Dwyryd.

Maentwrog, situated in a quiet corner of the Vale of Ffestiniog, consists of a cluster of grey stone, slate-roofed dwellings shaded by the steep afforested slopes of the Harlech Dome's foothills. Its name means the stone of Twrog. Twrog was a seventh century Celtic Christian and giant who was said to have hurled the sandstone pillar from the mountain above the village to the churchyard where it still stands. A more practical theory is that the stone was placed by the Romans to mark the intersection of two of their roads.

A country lane (starting at 665405) rises out of Maentwrog revealing excellent views of Moelwyn Bach's rugged southern face. If a right turn is made at the first junction and a left at the second this will lead to Bryntirion farm (680392) from where a track leads southwards to conifer plantations. The path converges with one from the Trawsfynydd Power Station before passing behind its reservoir's northern dam.

Trawsfynydd

Across the vast waters of Llyn Trawsfynydd the moorlands of the Migneint swell to the twin-peaked summit of Arenig Fawr. Much closer are the splintered knolls that rise to form the northern Rhinogs, which look like mountains stolen from a 'western' movie set.

The path, sketchy on this section, skirts the lake's shores over a leat, then through a field of bracken before joining a well-defined track above the oak copse of Coed y Rhygen. The path then rises to the shoulder of a rocky spur, Craig y Gwynt, which offers the best view of the lake, with the Moelwyns (Moelwyn Bach dominant), the Migneint, Arenig Fawr and Aran Fawddwy forming the east and northern horizons. For those who are opposed to nuclear power, and I number myself amongst them, the sight of the Trawsfynydd Station, set intrusively amongst attractive woodland, tempers the scene with a silent and invisible menace. This is sometimes accentuated by steam rising from the warm waters of the lake (see box). The path joins a narrow metalled lane on descending from Graig y Gwynt. A left turn at the junction a mile further on* will lead to the southern dam from where a long narrow footbridge crosses the reservoir to reach Trawsfynydd village.

* NB If camping on the mountains or on the moorlands north of the Coed-y-Brenin forest turn right at the junction and refer to the next chapter.

Trawsfynydd Nuclear Power Station standing beyond its steaming lake with the Moelwyn range in the background

TRAWSFYNYDD POWER STATION

Trawsfynydd's Power Station, completed in 1965, is of the early Magnox type. Encased in magnesium alloy cans are alternate rods of natural uranium fuel and graphite moderators (these enable the rate of fission to be controlled). The heat generated is carried by carbon dioxide gas which leaves the reactor at 396°C and this in turn is used to convert water into steam to drive the station's turbines.

The thirty-five million gallons of water per hour needed to cool the installation are drawn from the reservoir. The heated water is then forced around the perimeter of the lake before returning to the intakes.

The plant was originally rated at 500 megawatts but since the early seventies has been rated at only 300 megawatts. This lessens the effects of corrosion in and around the reactor core.

The safety record of Trawsfynydd has deteriorated. There has been a serious fire and many minor incidents such as accidental emissions of radioactive carbon dioxide and leaking safety valves. Much of the reason for concern over the station is that its inland siting and the use of a small lake for cooling does not allow the satisfactory dispersal of liquid radioactive wastes. Long-lived isotopes such as Americium and Plutonium have been detected in mud samples taken from the lake and there has been a rapid increase in radiation levels found in fish here.

Like many other Magnox power stations in Europe, Trawsfynydd has now exceeded its proposed lifespan of 20 years, and this has caused a great deal of worry to many respected scientists. In a BBC TV 'Brass Tacks' report by David Taylor it was suggested that the extension in the lifespan was granted for military rather than economic reasons and that the Plutonium produced as a fissile by-product was being processed for the manufacture of nuclear warheads.

There are proposals to build another nuclear power station on the site of the present one – this time a pressurised water reactor. However, for economic reasons, Wylfa on Anglesey has jumped the queue. In a statement the CEGB said that the lake at Trawsfynydd would have to be doubled in size flooding an area 'which is of some ecological importance'. The scheme will almost certainly be revived and it can only be hoped that it will be stoutly resisted.

Ascending Moelwyn Mawr with Moel-yr-hydd and Tanygrisiau in the background

The Festiniog railway near Dduallt

On Craigysgafn with Moelwyn Mawr beyond

THE HIGH MOUNTAIN ALTERNATIVE

Moelwyns

A route linking the peaks of Moelwyn Mawr and Bach involves an extra 1,100ft of ascent and would be a worthwhile exercise in clear conditions. It gains vantage points aloof from industrial incursions where the mountain reigns supreme.

Moelwyn Mawr

The mountain alternative diverges from the main route by the Rhosydd Quarry buildings (665463) where it passes to the west of the huge spoil heap to their rear and climbs south-westwards on grassy terrain to the northern shores of Llyn Croesor. The distinctive outlines of Cnicht are always prominent in views to the west.

A dam/causeway on the small reservoir's western edge is crossed before climbing southwards on a grassy spur to Moelwyn Mawr's summit, which is crowned with a stone trig point.

From the summit Snowdon, Moel Siabod, the Glyders, the Rhinogs and Cadair Idris can all be seen in distant panoramas, but the most impressive scene is that across the mountain's northern crags and scree to Cnicht, whose steep, scarred sides plunge to the depths of Cwm Croesor, sixteen hundred feet below.

The easy southern grass slopes of Moelwyn Mawr are rudely interrupted by the rough ridge of Craigysgafn and the descent to Bwlch Stwlan, the pass between the two Moelwyns, must be undertaken with care. Wide white veins of quartz are seen in the rocks. The view north-westwards from Bwlch Stwlan, a grassy col, encompasses the Stwlan reservoir, the cliffs of Ceseiliau Moelwyn (popular with climbers) and the grey town of Blaenau Ffestiniog surrounded by dismal, slate-terraced mountainsides.

Moelwyn Bach

A narrow track from Bwlch Stwlan rises on the north-eastern face of Moelwyn Bach, traversing screes before rising south-westwards on a grass slope to the summit, an airy, isolated plateau of grass with outcrops of rock.

In unbroken southern panoramas, the skyline includes, in the east, the Berwyns and Arans, whilst the more westerly Cadair Idris leads the eye to the graceful arc of Cardigan Bay. Beyond the Vale of Ffestiniog by the northern reaches of the Harlech Dome, is Llyn Trawsfynydd, with its nuclear power station on the western shore.

The route now described from the summit of Moelwyn Bach is not a recognised one and therefore there will be no evident tracks. Retrace your footsteps on the grassy eastern slopes until the prominent cliffs of Carreg Blaen-Llym come into view. An easterly course aiming for a point south of this feature will lead to the source of the Nant Ddu. Care will be needed in the initial stages when rocky shelves and knolls will have to be rounded. Follow the northern banks of the stream before crossing at the footbridge mentioned in the main route description (676438) and then continue along the same paths to Trawsfynydd.

If the visibility is poor it would be wiser to retrace steps to Bwlch Stwlan, descend to Llyn Stwlan and make for the dam from which point the descent is described in the main route section.

The view south from Moelwyn Mawr, over Craigysgafn to Moelwyn Bach with Trawsfynydd Power Station in the distance

Typical Rhinog countryside on the north-east side of Rhinog Fawr

CHAPTER 4

ROUTES THROUGH THE RHINOGS
TRAWSFYNYDD TO BARMOUTH

From the first steps out of Trawsfynydd village the magnetism of the Rhinogs is felt, hastening the march over the moorland which lies to their north-east and away from the power station and its polluted lake.

The range, which is more correctly known as the Harlech Dome and stretches twenty-two miles from Maentwrog to Barmouth, is particularly rugged and complex at its northern end, having the reputation of being the roughest terrain in Wales. It consists of thick beds of gritstone and shale formed in the Cambrian era. The much faulted rocks are riven by deep transverse canyons that create repeated obstacles to the hiker walking the 'ridge', and thus early roads, paths and tracks all ran east-west taking the natural lie of the land across the axis of the range. Boulders and scree from the eroded gritstone slabs are frequently covered with thigh-deep heather, making progress slow and treacherous. Craig Wion and all peaks to its north are extremes of this form and are, as such, particularly arduous for the backpacker.

Although dull by comparison, the section of the route I have chosen across the moorlands of Crawcwellt and the Coed-y-Brenin Forest offers a very quick passage to the 'big' Rhinogs, leaving time and energy to complete the journey to Barmouth within a single day.

An ancient track, which threads through Bwlch Drws Ardudwy – a narrow, heathery ravine between the sombre crags of Rhinogs Fawr and Fach – facilitates the low-level route, which also follows the course of the old London to Harlech Mail Coach Road from the Ysgethin Valley to the Llawlech Ridge.

Despite the extremely rough going, those who follow the high-level route will be rewarded with superb views, good scrambling on Rhinog Fawr, and the circuit around the dramatically situated Llyn Hywel, surely the finest mountain tarn in Wales. Once past Y Llethr the rough terrain relents: the heather and boulders are replaced by smooth grassy ridges which allow rapid, carefree progress.

At the southern end new vistas unfold. The Mawddach Estuary, described by Wordsworth as 'sublime' is seen at its best around Llawlech, included in both high and low-level routes.

Barmouth, the destination, lies on a narrow coastal strip beneath the fragmented cliffs of Garn, the last outpost of the Rhinogs. Here the smell of salt sea air mingles with the aroma from fish and chip shops and hamburger stalls.

Trawsfynydd

On leaving Trawsfynydd the route returns to the junction of minor roads near Tyndrain (696347) at the southern end of the lake and follows the left fork for about a mile until a road sign (687335) declares 'No footpaths beyond this point'. From here a south-west-bound cart track leads to the Afon Crawcwellt, which is crossed using a primitive slate-and-corrugated-iron footbridge leading to the abandoned farm of Wern-fach from where the path heads up the grassy slopes of Moel y

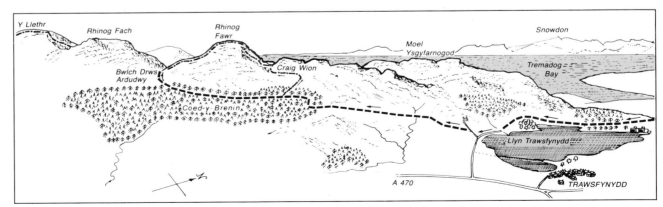

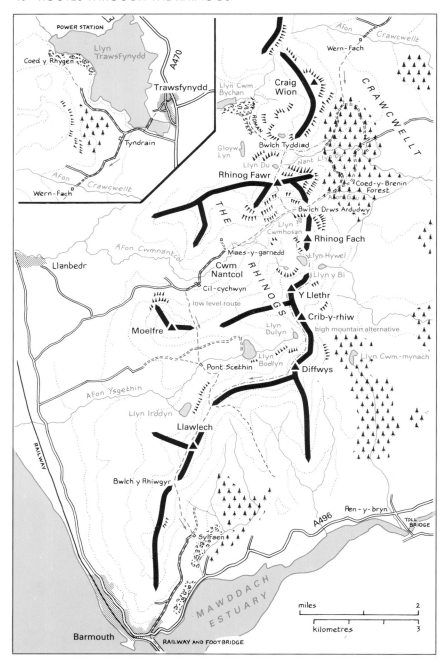

Approaching the Coed-y-Brenin Forest with Rhinog Fach and Rhinog Fawr beyond

Gwartheg. The path is waymarked by yellow arrows which are daubed on the fence-posts on the initial stages and later, as the path changes to a southerly course, on occasional rocks which become more abundant as altitude is gained.

Coed-y-Brenin Forest

The woods of Ffridd Maes-gwyn, part of the massive Coed-y-Brenin Plantations, lie directly ahead, whilst the oddly-profiled Craig Wion lures the gaze to the west. The forest is entered at a stile and more yellow arrows lead past

The old pack-horse bridge – Pont Scethin – on the Harlech to London road over the Rhinogs.

The Rhinog range from Llyn Trawsfynydd: (l to r) Diffwys, Y Llethr, Rhinog Fach and Rhinog Fawr

a ruined stone building to a Forestry Commission road which is followed southwards. At 670299, just north of where the road crosses the Nant Llyn du, the high and low-level routes diverge. Those who opt for the latter choice continue to a left fork half a mile to the south and thence to another junction and a bend where a path leads west-south-west along the northern bank of the Afon Gau.

Bwlch Drws Ardudwy

The regimented ranks of larch and spruce are now replaced by the tangled terrain of the lower Rhinog slopes. The way ahead is to Bwlch Drws Ardudwy, a rugged pass between Rhinogs Fawr and Fach, whose fissured crags rise from a rough seam of heather that is so typical of this range. The path is little more than a twelve-inch ribbon of compacted subsoil and rock through the thick heather, but it is always well-defined making it impossible to stray from the route. The Bwlch itself is a wild place. A rocky knoll rises from the base of the narrow gorge between the vying ramparts of the two Rhinog peaks and is marked with a large cairn.

Cwm Nantcol

From here the path descends Cwm Nantcol, where the wilderness is transformed into the green hues of cultivated land with the smoothly contoured Moelfre dominating the view ahead. The Cwm Nantcol road is joined at

Climbing southward on the old road out of the Ysgethin valley. Rhinog Fawr, Y Llethr are the peaks on the horizon with Llyn Bodlyn on the right

Maes-y-garnedd and this is followed until the public footpath sign beyond Cil-cychwyn farm points the way southwards over the grassy eastern arm of Moelfre.

The path (also waymarked) is slightly to the east of the one shown on Ordnance Survey maps and rises to the col between Moelfre and Y Llethr. From the ridge it will be noticed that the valley of Ysgethin, to the south, is more barren and featureless than that of Cwm Nantcol. Two lakes, Llyn Bodlyn and Llyn Irddyn lie beneath the sparsely-cragged, rounded hills of Diffwys and Llawlech respectively and the aura of this expansive, uninhabited valley is one of bleakness, making it easy to imagine the highway robberies that frequently took place in these parts. The ruins of an old inn, almost certainly frequented by the highwaymen, lie near to the small conifer copse at the southern foot of Moelfre. Here bandits once robbed a party of London gentlefolk who had halted at the inn on their way to attend a society wedding at Harlech.

The descent into the Ysgethin valley

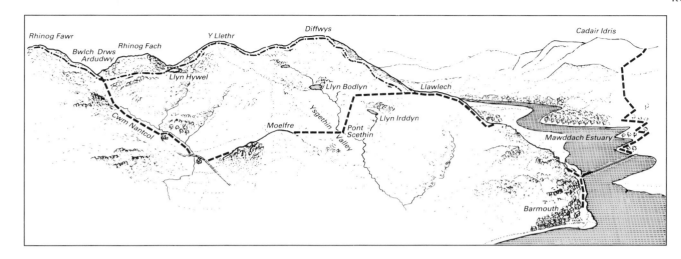

anglers. On reaching the ridge, the walker is rewarded with a fine prospect of the northern ramparts of Cadair Idris beyond the wide Mawddach Estuary.

The route now used follows the grassy ridge towards Barmouth, first rising to the summit of Llawlech and then descending to Bwlch y Rhiwgyr. Bwlch y Rhiwgyr, or Pass of the Horns, got its name from the bandit watchmen who at nightfall would lie in wait for potential victims. They would sound their horns when the unwary traveller, perhaps a drover returning with moneys, passed, thus alerting a nearby band. A tale by William Davies (1898) tells of a man who knew of these bandits but, hav-

The Afon Cwm Nantcol near Pont Cerrig

is trackless but a bearing of 200° (south-south-west) across rough grassland will lead to Pont Scethin, a small, stone pack-horse bridge which carried what was once the main highway between London and Harlech.

Llawlech

Beyond the well preserved little bridge the path veers to the south-east, indistinctly at first, but becoming quite prominent when raking acutely south-south-west up the steep slopes of Llawlech along the old London highway.

A little way up this hill lies Janet Haigh's Memorial Stone, which was erected by her son Melvyn, a Bishop of Winchester, after her death in 1953. It reads, 'To the enduring memory of Janet Haigh, who even as late as her eighty-fourth year despite dim sight and stiffened joints still loved to walk this way from Tal-y-Bont to Penmaenpool . . . Courage traveller'.

The ancient road continues above the western crags of Llawlech, beneath which lies the lonely lake, Llyn Irddyn, a favourite spot of many Cambrian

Rhinog Fawr's northern crags seen from Llyn Du

Sunset over Tremadog Bay from the summit of Rhinog Fawr

Rhinog Fach from Llyn Hywel

ing faith in the speed of his horse, still decided to continue over the Bwlch at night. On reaching the top he saw the shadow of a horseman through the murk and heard the shrill sound of a horn. Suddenly he was surrounded. He decided to try and escape and made his horse go faster up the hill. The bandits gave up the chase and the man arrived home safely, but the following morning when he went to the stables he found the horse dead – the effort had been too much.

It is possible to keep to the ridge beyond the Bwlch but the increasingly craggy hilltops are crossed by many high stone walls: progress over these will be slow and may cause damage to the environment. It is much better to descend the ancient drovers' route from the Bwlch to the whitewashed farm buildings of Sylfaen where a delightful country lane leads down to the sea at Barmouth.

THE HIGH MOUNTAIN ALTERNATIVE

Rhinog Fawr

The Rhinog mountain route is the toughest, roughest route in the book, and this is especially noticeable in the section north of Y Llethr. Here the hills know no gentle inclines but soar to the skyline in abrupt bluffs and buttresses often skirted by slippery screes and thick heather.

The divergence from the low-level is in the conifer plantations of Ffridd Maes gwyn by the Nant Llyn du. Instead of continuing along the forestry road, a right turn is made following a grassy path just north of the stream (670299). A stile marks the exit from the woods and the first intimate prospect of the big Rhinog is unfolded.

The vertical slabs of Rhinog Fawr tower above to your left, while ahead is the tiny path through the thickly heathered slopes leading to Bwlch Tyddiad and the famous 'Roman Steps'. The path to the Bwlch is followed until one leading southwards and directly towards Rhinog Fawr is reached (661299). This rocky path leads to Llyn Du, a desolate spot over which Rhinog Fawr's northern face glowers unrelentingly. However, a shelf that rises beneath a huge vertical wall of rock at the southeastern shore of the lake provides a start for the short, steep ascent which involves some scrambling. The summit is marked by a cairn and a trig point and is

adorned with a rich carpet of heather and bilberries, so different from the mountain slopes below. The view to the south is dominated by the huddled peaks of Rhinog Fach and Y Llethr whose craggy terraces cradle the high tarn of Llyn Hywel. To the north the eye can follow the horizon from the Lleyn Peninsular up a gradually rising mountain profile to Snowdon's five peaks. In an intimate north-western scene, two lakes, Llyn Cwm Bychan and Gloyw Lyn nestle beneath the much faulted gritstone outcrops of Carreg-y-saeth and Clip respectively.

The scramble from Rhinog Fawr summit to Bwlch Drws Ardudwy is rough but not dangerous providing due care is exercised, particularly in the west. There are many natural channels for the descent and although there are no obvious paths you will be on course if you keep approximately in line with Llyn Cwmhosan at the foot of Rhinog Fach. The Bwlch itself is usually quite boggy, especially by the wall that runs its length.

Llyn Hywel and Rhinog Fach

We are confronted by Rhinog Fach whose dark ramparts seem an obvious challenge, but one that I think should be ignored, for little is gained (views are inferior to those of Rhinog Fawr) and valuable time and energies are lost in its pursuit – especially as the alternative way is both logical and more dramatic.

A better course rises steadily, through the profuse heather, past Llyn Cwmhosan and the huge boulders at the foot of the smaller Rhinog, and upwards until Llyn Hywel is reached. Of all the places on the walk, this is for me the most enchanting and the most memorable. On one side is Rhinog Fach, with

Y Llethr and Llyn Hywel from the southern slopes of Rhinog Fach. Llyn Perfeddau is the smaller lake on the right

The spectacular view north from Y Llethr over Llyn Hywel showing the crags and scree of Rhinog Fach with Rhinog Fawr in the background

its rocky crest overlooking loose boul- dered slopes plunging to the lapping shores of the lake, whilst on the other is Y Llethr, displaying more greenery but ribbed with huge diagonal rock strata. The pattern is continued on the narrow connecting ridge where the gigantic slabs of Y Llethr rise out of Hywel's waters. Poor weather conditions render this vicinity wild and inhospitable but all the more impressive.

A way leads around the Rhinog side of Llyn Hywel and up to the ridge above, keeping left of the Y Llethr slabs on a path strewn with boulders. Those intent on climbing Rhinog Fach could possibly leave their heavy rucksacks here and scramble northwards up the bouldery wall-side path to its summit. The climb and the return journey would probably take about half an hour and make a pleasant diversion.

Y Llethr

From the col above the slabs to the summit of Y Llethr the path is steep, but as there are marvellous retrospective views of the lake and Rhinog Fach there are plenty of excuses for frequent stops.

As Y Llethr's summit is reached the terrain changes. The contortions and rough going of the Rhinogs are quite suddenly replaced by very welcome, smooth, grassy ridges and the walking becomes easier correspondingly, so that the remaining section of the range to Barmouth is a genuine ridge walk.

Diffwys

From Y Llethr there is a large wall running along the ridge and this is followed on the western side. The next peak is Diffwys and, providing the weather is reasonable, it should be clearly visible. To the left, nestling in some woods below, is a delightful lake, Llyn Cwm-mynach. If time is short, or perhaps the weather turns nasty, the ridge can be left by the course of an old mine tramway which descends to these woods from the knoll just before Diff-wys. A forestry road would then lead you to the A496 road to Pen-y-bryn. This would involve a major diversion from the described route via Barmouth. If this diversion is taken the best way to regain the main path would be to cross the Mawddach on the Penmaenpool Toll Bridge and go by road past the Kings Youth Hostel to Ty Nant (698152) where the Pony Path can be used to Cadair Idris. If the weather is good it is best to continue over Diffwys as the views from this peak are better than any

Looking south along the wall linking Y Llethr with Diffwys

At the summit of Diffwys

in the range. The whole Cadair Idris group can be seen to great advantage across the Mawddach Estuary and there should be an uninterrupted view of the graceful curve of Cardigan Bay.

From Diffwys the ridge curves to the west, descending to a pass south of Pont Scethin, where the mountain route converges with the lower-level path on the descent to Barmouth.

The view east from Barmouth past
the toll bridge to the Cadair Idris range

CHAPTER 5

CADAIR IDRIS AND THE TARRENS

BARMOUTH TO MACHYNLLETH

Whether you climb to its lofty summit or skirt its perimeters the massif of Cadair Idris will totally capture the centre stage of this section. In views from Barmouth's long bridge her proud precipices tower boldly above the wooded foothills that rise from the sands of the Mawddach Estuary, luring the walker in an irresistible challenge to set foot on her slopes.

The 'high' route explores Cadair's craggy cwms and gullies, passing through a mountainscape as magnificently sculpted as any in Wales. A different side to the mountain's character is revealed on the lower route,

when the gentle green slopes fall in graceful arcs to the valley of the Afon Cadair. Those who seek peaceful, secluded scenery will be in their element in this quiet corner of Cambria.

Beyond the slate-mining village of Abergynolwyn lie the little-frequented Tarren Hills which, although ravaged by extensive conifer planting, still retain their intrinsic wildness. These are the last outposts of the Snowdonia National Park, but they mark the beginnings of a phase of the journey – that of the Elenydd or Green Desert.

Mawddach Estuary

An exhilarating start to the day is provided by the walk across the Barmouth toll-bridge which commands extensive views along the Mawddach Estuary to the hills of Cadair Idris and Diffwys.

The half-mile-long viaduct, built in 1860 by the Welsh Coast Railway Company, is constructed from wood except for the part which spans the river's main Channel. Here a four-hundred-foot steel section, part of which swings open to allow the passage of ships, is supported by huge cylinders which were driven 120 feet through alluvial deposits to penetrate the firm rock below. One side of the bridge carries the Cambrian Coast Railway linking Aberystwyth and Pwllheli and the other a delightfully convenient footbridge.

On crossing the estuary, a footpath leads eastwards at the river's edge and skirts the wooded slopes of the diminutive knoll of Fegla Fawr. After passing

to the south of a small group of terraced cottages, our route diverges from the riverside walk at 633149 and heads south-east, passing some allotments and a disused railway line, to the A493 road and Arthog just to the east.

Cregennen Lakes

From Arthog follow a lane signposted 'Cregennen Lakes'. This gated little lane winds its way up the western foothills of Cadair Idris and provides wonderful views across the Mawddach Estuary to

Barmouth, before levelling out on reaching the shores of Llynnau Cregennen. The two small lakes are dominated by the cliffs of the northern face of Tyrrau Mawr.

A road junction is encountered just

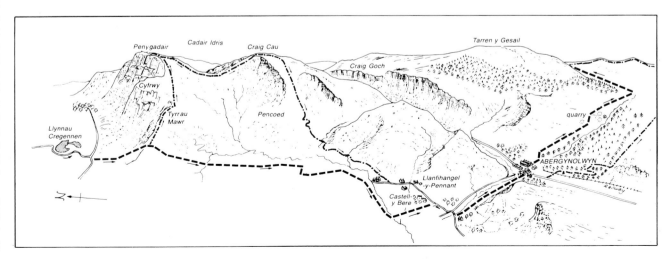

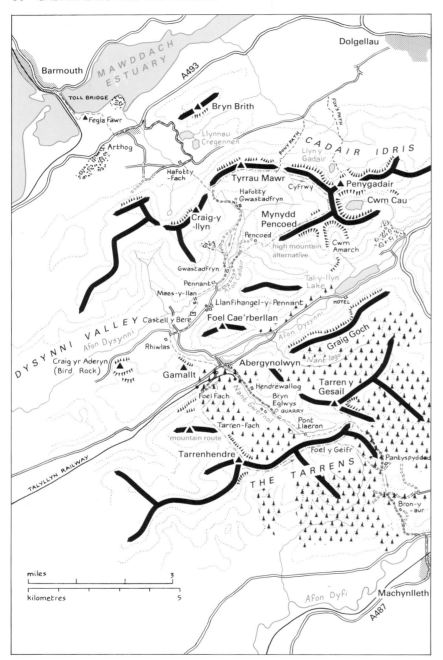

Tyrrau Mawr from Llynnau Cregennen

beyond the lakes and, after a short walk, a track heading into the mountains is located opposite a ruined farmstead, Hafotty-fach. After crossing two stiles, steep grassy slopes must be climbed to reach a pass at the lowest point of the ridge west of the summit of Tyrrau Mawr. This too is a splendid viewpoint. In the foreground, but far below, lie the two lakes of Cregennen, nestling beneath Bryn Brith's bold, rocky flanks. Across the Mawddach the descending ridge from Diffwys to the sea leads the eye to Barmouth, its far-reaching sand bars, and the long bridge spanning the estuary.

The Valley of Afon Cadair

Just beyond the electric fence which runs along the ridge top and is scaled by a wooden stile, a right turn is made along a newly-constructed farm road which descends into the green valley of the Afon Cadair which has a surprisingly pastoral character that barely hints at its proximity to the craggy higher cwms of the Cadair massif less than two miles to the east.

The flinted track descends to Gwast-adfryn farm where there is a delightful campsite next to the sprightly, tree-lined river. A small detour over the Cadair Bridge at Pennant farm (673096) (un-named on the 1:50,000 map) will enable you to see the ruins of Tyn-y-ddol. Here stands a monument to a poor girl, Mary Jones, who walked twenty-five miles barefoot to the home of Thomas Charles at Bala in order to purchase a copy of the Bible – an act that is reputed to have inspired the formation of the British and Foreign Bible Society.

Beyond Pennant farm the route keeps to the Afon Cadair's northern bank until it crosses at the footbridge near Maes-y-llan farm (666091) and heads south across fields towards the western edge of a rock outcrop on which the fortress Castell y Bere is perched. From here Prince Llewelyn-ap-Gruffydd stoutly resisted the armies of Edward I until, in 1283, he was finally defeated.

In the Dysynni valley, a curiously-profiled rocky protuberance, Craig yr Aderyn (Bird Rock) juts out from the gentle, verdant neighbouring hills. The crag's upper section is a breeding ground for cormorants, one of the very few inland sites in the British Isles. The steep lower facet, close to the road, boasts a plethora of very difficult rock climbs.

The path meets a narrow country lane west of Llanfihangel-y-Pennant. At this point the best course is to follow the lane south-westwards to the farm of Rhiwlas (660078) by Pont Ystumanner.

Abergynolwyn

From Rhiwlas a lovely path heads back south-east above the Afon Dysynni where it cuts through a narrow valley between Gamallt and Foel Cae'rberllan. Abergynolwyn is strategically placed where the valley opens out. On the other side of Abergynolwyn the Tarren Mountains bar the way to Machynlleth.

The village, which originally relied on the quarrying activities, now thrives on the tourism brought by the Talyllyn narrow gauge railway, and on work provided by the Forestry Commission whose plantations cloak the slopes of the Tarren mountains to the south.

Nant Gwernol

The expanding clutches of the monotonous conifer forests are all too evident in the valley of the Nant Gwernol that leads south-east from Abergynolwyn, threatening to submerge even the two-thousand-foot hills of Tarrenhendre and Tarren y Gesail.

Nant Gwernol, which is also known as 'The Wild Ravine', is entered from Pandy Square, opposite the Railway Inn where a metalled lane rises up the south-

The view to the Dysynni Valley from Mynydd Pencoed

The ruins of Castell y Bere with Bird Rock profiled in the distance

The track leading up through the Tarren forests with the Cadair Idris range beyond

west slopes of Foel-y-Pandy (un-named on the 1:50,000 map) passing Hendrewallog farm before reaching the area of disused mines and quarries at Bryn-Eglwys.

Many relics of the bygone quarrying industry are seen here, in an area devastated by slag heaps and mine shafts. (These shafts are in particularly poor condition and exploring their depths is not recommended.)

After passing close to a huge quarry pit on the left, a signed footpath (694056) – not marked on the 1:50,000 map) leads off the track north-eastwards through infant spruce. About fifty yards further on it resumes its south-easterly course past the well-preserved pulley house above the Beudnewydd Incline. (On these inclines pulley-driven trucks would carry slate from the mines to the valley floor.) A collapsed chamber can be seen to the west and into its murky recesses tumble two streams forming fifty-foot waterfalls.

Beyond the incline the well-defined

The old quarry pulley house on the slopes of Tarren y Gesail

Pont Llaeron on the slopes of Foel y Geifr

grassy path, which can be marshy in places, rises above the old reservoir, now dry due to its dam being breached.

Foel y Geifr

On the slopes of Foel y Geifr ahead are new plantations (the trees were less than a foot tall in 1987). Nant Gwernol turns to the east below the slopes of Foel y Geifr and is crossed, using the ancient packhorse bridge, Pont Llaeron, said to be of Roman origin. Beyond, the path rises to the top of the pass between Tarren y Gesail, the tallest of the Tarren range, and the summit of Foel y Geifr (719056).

From here it descends slightly, and after a hundred yards turns southwards, crossing a fence via a primitive stile before joining a forestry track which descends on a south-westerly course through more spruce saplings passing south of spot height 332m (727046) before reaching the ruins of Pantyspyd-ded (728041). This is an important land-mark as it is here that we diverge from what would seem to be the obvious route (the forestry road). The less dist-inct path, occasionally waymarked with yellow arrows, leading south into the nearby forest is the correct one. After half a mile this path (not marked on the OS maps) meets four others at 729033. The forestry road to be used on this occasion is the one directly ahead and leading south-eastwards for a third of a mile before reaching the plantation's edge to the east of spot height 225m. The 'green road' that follows is a joy to descend, with airy views of the hills of Maesglase, Mynyddy Cemais and Plyn-limon beyond the brilliant green fields of the Dyfi Valley. The track, tree-lined in the lower stages, meets a narrow tarmac lane by a house, Cwm-glia (736023 – not marked on 1:50,000 map), and this leads to the A493 at Penrhyn Dyfi, just west of

The summit of Cadair Idris: Penygadair from Cyfrwy

the Dyfi Bridge, which marks the south-ern boundary of Snowdonia National Park. Half a mile to the south lies the busy little market town of Machynlleth dominated by its ornate Victorian clock-tower, the focal point of this section of the route – the heart of Mid Wales.

THE HIGH MOUNTAIN ALTERNATIVE

Cadair Idris

In terms of mountain architecture, Cadair Idris's majesty is second only to Snowdon's and the high-level traverse of its peaks has to rank as one of the highlights of this long walk. If it is undertaken, only the very fittest will be able to traverse the mountain, cross the Tarren's mountain route and reach Machynlleth in one day and it would therefore be wise to plan a break at Abergynolwyn.

Tyrrau Mawr

The mountain route breaks away from the low-level route on the ridge to the west of Tyrrau Mawr, which is the first summit visited – the way guided by a fence running along the edge of the precipitous Craig-las cliffs. From the summit of Tyrrau Mawr views of the northern landscape are similar to those described from the pass above Hafotty-fach, although the mountains of Snow-donia are added to the scene. A glance to the east reveals the highest point of Cadair Idris, beyond Cyfrwy. To the south the Afon Cadair descends beneath Mynydd Pencoed, threading its way between some lesser hills towards Llan-fihangel. The landscape hereabouts is more akin to moorland than mountain but, within two miles, this character totally changes, the contrast greatly enhancing the appeal of this mountain traverse.

Penygadair

The route from Tyrrau Mawr to Peny-gadair is straightforward. It meets the Pony Path at Rhiw Gwredydd, where you will probably be joined by other travelling companions on a well-used track to the summit. This leaves the

*Looking west to Cwfrwy and
Tyrrau Mawr from Penygadair*

Cwm Cau and Craig Cau from Penygadair

cliffs' edge beyond Rhiw Gwredydd and rises on the southern shoulder of Cyfrwy until just before the last stretch to the major peak, where the magnificent rock sculptures of its northern face are revealed. At its foot is the apple-shaped tarn Llyn y Gadair, which is also flanked by the rock crested scree slopes of Cyfrwy. It is from this cwm that the rough Fox's Path works its way up steep, scree-strewn slopes.

The bouldered summit of Penygadair commands excellent views of Snowdonia's skyline, with the Arans prominent to the north-east. To the south, beyond the rounded Tarrens, Plynlimon (more correctly termed Pumlumon) rises above its moorland satellites.

There is a covered shelter just below the summit for those who are unlucky enough to encounter bad weather.

Mynydd Pencoed

Our route from Penygadair now heads south-west, skirting above the immense precipices surrounding Llyn Cau. As it descends, the views of the fine cwm enclosing this tarn become more spectacular, especially at the top of Great Gully which splits the vertical cliffs of Craig-y-Cau. From the col the route ascends towards Craig-y-Cau (710122) but veers south-westwards just short of its summit, following the ridge-fence of Mynydd Pencoed. It traces the edge of the crag-rimmed Cwm Amarch, which directs the gaze down to the gleaming lake of Tal-y-llyn in the Dysynni valley, far below. On the opposite shores of the lake the diminutive, white-walled Ty'n-y-Cornel Hotel is dwarfed by the steep slopes of Graig Goch beyond.

Further along the ridge from Cwm Amarch is the summit of Mynydd Pencoed. From there the grassy western flank is descended to the old Pencoed farmhouse where the path leads to a farm road which fords the Nant Pencoed. A quarter of a mile further south a path to the right of the farm road goes down to the Afon Cadair, which it crosses via a footbridge and converges with the main route just north of Gwastadfryn farm.

THE TARREN MOUNTAIN ALTERNATIVE

Tarrenhendre

The main peaks of the Tarren range can be climbed in a horseshoe route around Cwm Gwernol south of Abergynolwyn, linking up with the second stage of the low-level route late in the day. The

Ascending the flank of the plantations on Tarren-fach above Abergynolwyn

conifer-cloaked Graig Goch.

Ahead is Tarrenhendre, a rounded, grass-covered peak ending abruptly at the chiselled north-eastern crags above the forest line. The final ascent to this summit is steep but the airy situation and the magnificent succeeding ridge-walk make the efforts worthwhile. In sunny, breezy weather there is an abundant variety of grasses hereabouts, enhancing the gentle slopes with an attractive blend of subtle hues.

The view to the south is now dominated by the meandering Dyfi as it widens amidst huge sandbanks to meet the sea. Across the estuary lie the flat peat bogs of Cors Fochno, now a nature reserve and habitat of many rare species of plant, insect and sea-bird. Further distant to the south-east, Pumlumon rises from the rolling hills south of Machynlleth.

Tarren y Gesail

From Tarrenhendre's summit the route now turns sharply to the east by a ridge which leads towards Foel y Geifr at the head of the 'Wild Ravine'. At this stage, if you have time in hand, continue along the ridge until the pass between Foel y Geifr and Tarren y Gesail is reached and then ascend the latter peak on a grassy spur with crags to the right. Insect-eating Sundew are amongst the interesting range of plants on this summit. Views down to Nant Iago and the precipitous crags guarding the exit into the Dysynni Valley are magnificent.

After the ascent of Tarren y Gesail retrace the route to the previously mentioned pass, where the main low-level route is joined on a descending track to Pantyspydded farm.

If time is pressing, the ascent of Tarren y Gesail can be omitted and after descending the Foel y Geifr ridge the low-level route may be joined at 719055.

mountain alternative is particularly arduous, the Tarren's slopes being steep-sided and grassy – the sort of terrain that really hurts the calf muscles. However these wild and lonely hills offer lovely views of Cadair Idris and the Dyfi Estuary. From just west of Abergynolwyn a forestry road leaves the B4405 at 674068, passes Hendre farm, and crosses the Talyllyn Railway before entering the plantations. After a right turn (west) at the first junction of forestry roads, the large flinted road

makes a 'U' turn as it gently climbs the slopes of Foel Fach. At 676064 an old dilapidated stone wall marks the inconspicuous start of an overgrown footpath, which doubles back to assume a south-westerly course. The path follows the wall, passing a ruined dwelling before veering left up a grassy tract. This widens about a hundred yards further on and, at this point, an old forestry track on the right-hand side is followed to the forest's edge, marked by a gate.

The next complex section is made

more confusing than normal by the need to switch to a new map (135) to the north of Tarrenhendre then, on its east, revert to the old one (124), for a short while. Constant changes in the extent of the plantation boundaries compound the problem.

The route now traces the edge of the plantations ascending north-eastwards on steep grassy slopes above Mynydd Pentre towards Tarren-fach (on the southern edge of map 124). Views to the left include Cadair Idris rising above the

Cadair Idris from Tarrenhendre

The final slope to the summit of Tarren y Gesail

The southern slopes of the Tarrens from above Pantyspydded

Looking east from Pumlumon Fawr to Pen Pumlumon Arwystli

CHAPTER 6

HYDDGEN AND PUMLUMON
MACHYNLLETH TO PANT MAWR

With the great peaks of Snowdonia behind us, beyond Machynlleth new landscapes unfold – less dramatic perhaps, but the contrast is nonetheless pleasant and stimulating.

The rounded, green Silurian hills are breached by a maze of valleys – narrow slivers of verdant pasture and hedgerow flanked by steep, thickly wooded slopes. In the initial stages the heads of many such vales are passed before the route rises to the subtle-hued, windswept peaks of Hyddgen and the Northern Elenydd. South of the majestic, scree-girt cliffs of Creigiau Bwlch Hyddgen the hills become bare and seem much loftier than the map suggests. We are now truly in the midst of a wild, remote area long since deserted by the rugged sheep farmers.

Pumlumon Fawr, often referred to as Plynlimon, has been unfairly described as 'a sodden weariness'. Most guidebooks only include the ascent from Eisteddfa Gurig via the old mines, probably the dullest route available. Take no notice! Pumlumon is a noble mountain, the highest in Central Wales and certainly the best vantage point to see both the north and south of the country. Being the birthplace of three great rivers, the Severn, the Wye and the Rheidol, it has its marshy places, but none on our route from the north, which takes in the beautiful glaciated cwm where dark Ordovician crags encircle the secluded tarn, Llyn Llygad Rheidol.

The easy descent is comforting, coming as it does at the end of the day, and it is good to know that if you are too late for beefburger and chips at the Eisteddfa Gurig cafe at least then you will be in time for a pint at the Glansevern Arms, Pant Mawr.

Machynlleth

From the busy streets of Machynlleth the Llyn Clywedog/Llanidloes mountain road leads south-eastwards towards the wild and desolate Elenydd Hills, sometimes known as the Green Desert.

At 754007 a signposted footpath crosses the town's golf course before zig-zagging up the steep, bracken-covered slopes of Parc from where impressive northern panoramas are revealed. Machynlleth, its clock tower protruding from the slate-grey rooftops, is sheltered by a small, partially afforested hill. Beyond the emerald fields of the Dyfi Valley rise the pale Tarren Hills whose smooth contours are rudely distorted by the patchwork plantations of spruce and larch.

The Rheidol Forest is entered at

Entering the Rhiw Goch plantations south of Hendre

756995 north of Llyn Glanmerin. The eastbound track, which gently curves to assume a southerly course, is in places overgrown and tightly enclosed by the crowded legions of spruce.

Bwlch

A five-bar gate marks the exit from the forest, and the path descends steeply to the lush meadows of a pass to the north of Bwlch farm. Hereabouts in spring the scene is transformed by brilliant splashes of colour added by the bluebells which grow in profusion.

From the pass the path climbs westwards along a tree-lined hollow offering, in its upper reaches, a view of Llyn Glanmerin at the head of the valley to the north. A track rises south-eastwards to the west of Bwlch farm and passes a small copse before reaching the open

The head of Cwm Hengwm with the Pumlumon massif in the distance

The descent to Hyddgen from Bwlch Hengwm

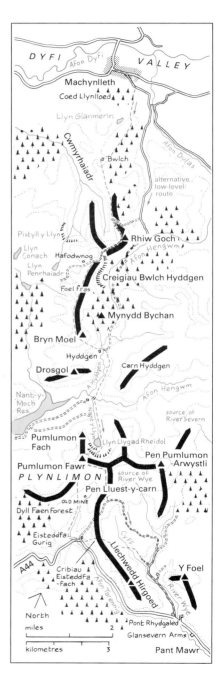

fellsides high above Cwmyrhaiadr, a deep sylvan valley. Prominent in views to the south, Pistyll y Llyn, a spout-like cascade, tumbles three hundred feet down a crag-rimmed cwm.

Creigiau Bwlch Hyddgen
Following a short descent, the route enters the Rhiw Goch plantations using a forestry road which heads south, close to Rhiw Goch's pointed summit. On leaving the forest on a stony track along the sharp north-east ridge, one of the walk's grandest landscapes is presented. Amongst precipitous, dark, vegetated crags the Afon Hengwm plunges, a foaming torrent, into a huge, heavily afforested basin. Above the forest line on the cwm's western side are vast, sweeping screes, crested by the cliffs of Creigiau Bwlch Hyddgen. On the southern skyline, beyond a coniferous sea, is Pumlumon whose fine northern aspect promises much. To the east its bare ochre foothills, divided by a complex system of glaciated valleys, are sparsely decorated with rocky cwms. There is a division of tracks at 765938. A right fork leads to Hafodwnog farm but the one used continues southwards on an undulating, grassy plateau above the cliffs at Creigiau Bwlch Hyddgen.

It is difficult to imagine Bwlch Hyddgen as anything other than a tranquil place far from the world's troubles but it was once the scene of a terrible battle – that of Nant Hyddgant (1401). On the slopes leading down to Hyddgen the English forces of Henry IV were slaughtered by those of Owain Glyndwr, Prince of Wales.

Hyddgen
South-east of Foel fras at 768922 the track which enters the forest near Mynydd Bychan is quitted for a less distinct path which winds around Bryn Moel before a descent is made on a trackless

course down its south-eastern slopes to the sheep-shearing sheds and ruins of Hyddgen, the scene of a tragic tale.

Locals often tell the story of a shepherd who was caught in a violent blizzard whilst working above Creigiau Bwlch Hyddgen. After making strenuous efforts to return to his farm at Hyddgen he collapsed with fatigue. His wife was alerted when his work-horse returned alone. Fearing the worst she took a lamp, for it was now dark, and searched for her husband. Finding him unconscious, she attempted to drag him back to their home, but her supreme efforts proved unsuccessful and both died on that ferocious night.

It is said that at the end of the day a light can be seen wavering as it travels from the valley to the spot where the shepherd fell. The spot was marked by neighbours with a ring of white stones

Camping by the Afon Hengwm under the northern slopes of Pumlumon

The sheep-shearing sheds at Hyddgen

Heading south down the valley of the Afon Hyddgen towards the Nant-y-Moch reservoir. It was hereabouts that Glyndwr's forces defeated the English in the Battle of Nant Hyddgant.

and, although most are scattered, those that remain can be seen from a nearby forestry road.

Pumlumon Fawr

From Hyddgen the route continues south-east, then south along the western flank of Carn Hyddgen. At the foot of Pumlumon, the valleys of the Hyddgen and Hengwm meet and the eastern tip of the huge Nant-y-moch Reservoir comes into view. The Afon Hengwm (not the same river encountered at Cwm

Hengwm) is crossed using a little concrete bridge to the east of the path. From here the Nant y Llyn is followed on its eastern bank to its source, Llyn Llygad Rheidol, an impressively-situated tarn crowded by the mountain's forbidding Ordovician cliffs. After circling the east and south shores of the tarn, high grassy corridors lead up to the pass between Pumlumon Fawr and Fach from where a simple south-southeasterly ascent leads to the stony summit

adorned with two large cairns, a trig point and a couple of shelters.

Being the highest mountain in the Elenydd region of Wales, Pumlumon Fawr has extensive and interesting vistas in all directions. The graceful arc of Cardigan Bay can be traced from the Lleyn Peninsular to the northern Pembrokeshire coast. Cadair Idris stands out boldly in front of the pale profiles of the distant Snowdonian giants in the north whilst, in the south, the great sandstone

escarpments of the Brecon Beacons and Carmarthen Fan can be clearly distinguished in good conditions. At Pumlumon's western foot the Nant-y-moch Reservoir and dam can be seen in their entirety amidst a mix of bare hills and spruce woods. The scheme was completed in 1963 and is part of the Central Electricity Generating Board's Cwm Rheidol Hydroelectric Scheme.

I have included two descents from Pumlumon's summit. The first has

Llyn Llygad Rheidol and Pumlumon Fawr

The summit rocks of Pumlumon Fawr

greater scenic merit and is more direct, whereas the second is easier to follow in poor weather.

Descent via Pen Lluest-y-carn
By descending eastwards guided by a ridge fence, Pumlumon's finest view, across Llyn Llygad Rheidol towards Hyddgen and Cadair Idris, can be seen. From this angle the cwm's magnificent architecture can be best appreciated. I can remember arriving here at first light on a February morning and being trans-fixed by the scene. A translucent, pinkish light penetrated the early haze, accen-tuating the russet mountain grasses and lending an air of mystery to the view in which the unlit north-facing crags still retained a light sprinkling of snow from previous falls. It would be worth camp-ing high on the mountain to see such a spectacle.

The path rises on the grassy shoulder of a peak defined by Phil Cooper in *The Big Walks* as Pen Pumlumon Llygad-

Bychan (not marked on 1:50,000 maps), before descending southwards, still guided by a fence, to Pen Lluest-y-carn. A five-bar gate in the fence marks the

spot where a descent to a newly con-structed farm road must be made (shown on 1:50,000 maps after 1986). It is clearly visible from the gate in clear

conditions but in low cloud or hill fog a south-easterly course should be taken before turning left along the road which, after rounding the head of Cyff, descends

The view west from Pumlumon Fawr towards the Nant-y-Moch reservoir

The Eisteddfa Gurig farm/cafe beneath the southern slopes of Pumlumon

south-east to the Wye Valley. To the north the wide, barren valley of the upper Wye can be seen close to its source. In distant views to the south-east the more fertile valleys of the Wye at Pant Mawr, and its tributary the Tarennig, give relief to the monochrome but not unappealing moorland scenery.

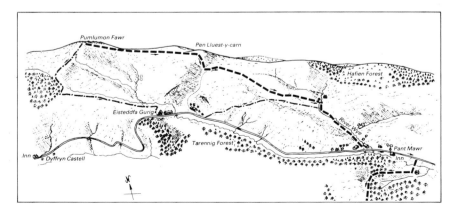

The crossing of the Wye (825848) can be a little tricky after periods of heavy rain. Once over the river a right turn along a forest/farm road follows the Wye's narrow valley to the A44 at Pont Rhydgaled farm (named Bontrhydgaled on pre 1986 maps), half a mile west of the Glansevern Arms.

Descent via Eisteddfa Gurig

From the summit of Pumlumon the route normally described in guidebooks descends to the old mines to the south-east and is very dull indeed. A far better alternative is to follow Pumlumon's southern ridge where the walking on a gentle grassy incline is easy and includes airy views.

The perimeters of a forest at Dyll Faen are followed until a bridleway is encountered (787841). Here a descent eastwards on rougher, tussocky grass is guided by a fence to the old mine road just west of the farm at Eisteddfa Gurig. Many will want to stop at the farm, which offers bed and breakfast and caters for campers (there is also a good cafe here). Those wishing to continue to the Glansevern Arms at Pant Mawr can either do so by following the A44 for three and a half miles, or take a slightly more circuitous hill route following a path over Cribiau Eisteddfa-fach (mis-spelt on the 1:50,000 maps). This ascent is easy on short grazed grassy slopes and from the top is is possible to discern the clearing in the massive Tarennig Forest to the south-east where the Roman fort, Cae Gaer, once stood. After descending the northern slopes to cross the stream called Cyff the path rises to a farm track, which crosses the River Wye south of Y Drum and thence the first route to Pont Rhydgaled farm may be followed.

A NOTE ON ACCOMMODATION

The Dyffryn Castell Hotel to the west (774817) offers fine alternative accommodation although it would involve a little road walking, or a route variation on the following day, to return to the described itinerary. From the side of the Dyll Faen forest, instead of descending eastwards at 787841 on the Eisteddfa Gurig route, continue south-westwards on a path which leads directly to the hotel on steep grassy slopes. The village of Ponterwyd is just two miles further west on the banks of the Rheidol.

CHAPTER 7

THE GREAT RESERVOIRS
PANT MAWR TO ELAN VILLAGE

This section of the route begins with unexciting forestry slopes but ends with a splendid excursion above the impressive reservoirs and dams of the Elan Valley. Marred by the scars of mass afforestation the hillside south of the Wye Valley promises little, but the mood changes on the gritstone outcrops of Craig y Lluest, where views of the glaciated Ystwyth Valley to its west raise the spirits for the continuation down the desolate wastelands of High Elan.

Beyond Pont ar Elan, the expansive quiet waters of the Craig Goch Reservoir add a serenity to the landscape. Nature has harmonised its ageing artificial shores, now over eighty years old, with their surroundings. The tranquillity of the scene is rudely interrupted at the dam where the overspill thunderously cascades as a white wall of water into the forested valley below. The power and presence of the Elan Dams is an awe-inspiring sight which, though massively intrusive, curiously adds great character to the landscape.

South of Craig Goch, the contours converge and gritstone crags protrude above gorge-like valleys. Rock enthusiasts could not fail to be impressed by the cliffs of Graig Dolfaenog which rise precipitously from the wooded slopes above the Carreg-ddu Reservoir, nor by Craig y Foel, north of the Caban-coch Reservoir.

The path that rises from Carreg-ddu to Y Glog Fawr gives memorable and contrasting views of both the Wye and Lower Elan Valleys before descending easily through a green and gentle landscape to the terminus at Elan Village.

Pant Mawr

To reach the Elan Valley the high, forestry-clad fells to the south of the Wye Valley must be scaled. The path starts inconspicuously about four hundred yards east of the Glansevern Inn on the A44. It is not signposted, but is easily pinpointed by its position opposite a wooden footbridge (854821) spanning the River Wye, which meanders through flat green fields at the edge of the unsightly, half-felled plantations of the Tarennig Forest. The path utilises the rickety old footbridge before heading southwards across the fields to the stone-built farmhouse of Nanty, surrounded by stands of spruce and larch.

Bryn Du

A left turn along a track by the farm leads to a Forestry Commission road

The east shores of the Craig Goch reservoir

which ascends the northern side of the valley westwards and then south-west to gain the ridge at Bryn Du (843807), where it briefly enters open fellside, giving views of Pumlumon on the northern horizon. The bridleway which follows the crest of the ridge is not navigable due to the Forestry Commisson's overplanting within their boundaries, and neither waymarking nor providing stiles over barbed wire perimeter fences. Shortly after re-entering the forest the path descends to cross the Afon Diliw close to the ruins of Nant Rhys. It then follows the widening and increasingly lively river which it fords just past the plantation's edge.

Craig y Lluest

A southbound path passes east of the old farm buildings of Lluest-dolgwiail be-

The head of the Ystwyth Valley from Craig y Lluest

Craig y Lluest and the great marsh of Gors Lwyd at the watershed between the Ystwyth and Elan Valleys

fore rising up the steep grassy slopes towards Craig y Lluest. The path is little used and indistinct. Once the ridge is attained it is preferable to head southwards to the rock outcrops (849759) in order to see striking views down the Ystwyth valley towards the lead mines of Cwmystwyth. Two fine, craggy hanging valleys, Craig Cwmtinwen and Graig Ddu, interrupt the sweeping lines of the grass and bracken clad hills that surround the river, which has cut a deep, craggy bed through their thin topsoils. A narrow tarmac ribbon, the Cwmystwyth to Rhayader mountain road, twists along the southern side of the valley before fading from view beyond the mine ruins. An equally impressive view is seen northwards along the Diliw Valley where Pumlumon forms the skyline.

The Upper Elan Valley

From Craig y Lluest a steep descent is made to the point where the mountain road bends south-east towards the Elan Valley. A wooden bridge is used to cross the now shallow Ystwyth. A great marsh, Gors Lwyd, lies between the two rivers. Here the Ystwyth is slowly stealing the waters of the Elan in an excellent example of river capture, a process which will take millions of years to evolve.

The mountain road is used for a quick and easy passage through the barren and scruffy landscapes of the wide upper Elan Valley passing Bodtalog, once the scene of a turnpike fracas of the Rebecca Riots. On the night of October 9th, 1843 an old lady who collected tolls there was set upon by the rioters, one of whom fired a powder gun directly at her face injuring both eyes. Although able to identify her attackers she refused to do so in spite of the offer of a £50 reward for information. The fear of reprisal was too great – such was the vehemence of the

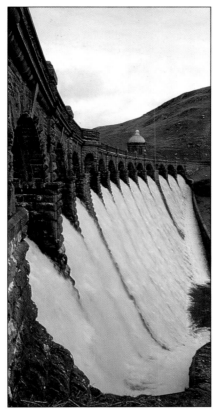

The Craig Goch Dam

The view back to the Craig Goch Dam from the Penygarreg reservoir.

Rebeccas. This area was recently the site of a proposed enlargement of the Craig Goch Reservoir, a scheme which was shelved (permanently I hope!).

Craig Goch Reservoir

The mountain road is left where it converges with the reservoir road which twists and rapidly descends to Pont ar Elan at the head of the Craig Goch Reservoir. From here a course along the eastern shores of the lake across wettish rough grassland, keeping to the left of the Water Board fence, leads to a wide, grassy cart track which rises high above the lakeshore. Craig Goch is more secluded than its neighbours and encircled by barren, featureless grassy hills. However its lack of physical character is outweighed by its tranquillity and its indefinable, ethereal qualities.

After passing a ruined cottage the track becomes less well-defined until it is joined by a green road from the ridge, Esgair Perfedd. It then descends to the massive Craig Goch Dam where the head of water cascades thunderously under thirteen arches to the river below.

Penygarreg Reservoir

The barren hills, now craggy in places, close in on the L-shaped Penygarreg Reservoir. The moorland is now partially wooded, coniferous to the south and broad-leaved to the north.

A stony track follows the eastern and then northern shores of the lake before reaching the next dam. From here, in the view to the east, expansive scree and cliffs tower to the skyline in a very impressive scene. This is Graig Dolfaenog.

Carreg-ddu Reservoir

At the northern extremity of the Carreg-ddu Reservoir a grassy track descends

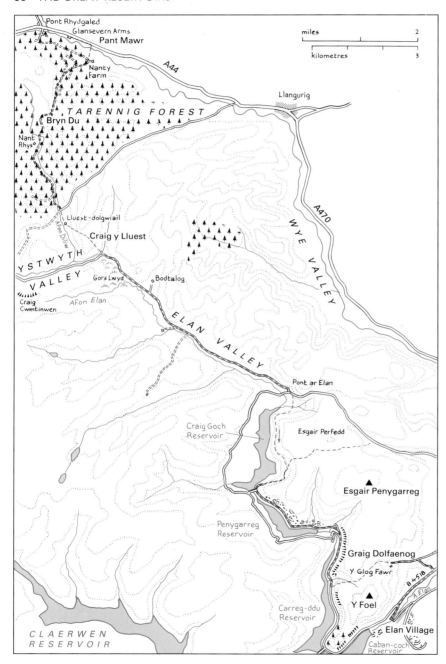

THE ELAN VALLEY RESERVOIR

The Birmingham Corporation Water Act of 1892 permitted the construction of reservoirs in the Elan and Claerwen Valleys, which would satisfy the ever-growing demands for water by the city's industries.

In the first part of the scheme four reservoirs, namely Craig Goch, Penygarreg, Carreg-ddu and Caban-coch were constructed in the Elan Valley, producing a combined capacity of 11,000 million gallons.

Filter beds were built east of the Caban Reservoir in order to extract the peat which would in time have blocked the seventy-three-mile pipeline to the Franklin Storage Reservoir near Birmingham. The water flows the whole distance on this inclined pipeline under the forces of gravity.

A novel feature of the scheme helps preserve water supplies in times of drought. Between the reservoirs of Carreg-ddu and Caban-coch is a dam submerged forty feet below the high water level (above it a bridge conveys the motor road to Claerwen). Adjacent on the upstream side of the dam is the Foel Tower where water is drawn and conveyed by tunnel to the filter beds. The submerged dam helps maintain a level sufficient to keep the Foel Tunnel charged with water, whilst the lower Caban-coch lake would be used to discharge into the Afon Elan the mandatory twenty-nine thousand gallons a day required to keep the ecological status quo. The Dolymynach tunnel, whose inlet is near to an unfinished dam at the western end of Caban-coch also supplements the Carreg-ddu levels by diverting to that reservoir (in times of drought) supplies from the Claerwen which would normally flow to Caban-coch.

Work commenced on the scheme in 1893 when a railway to supply men and materials to the sites of the dams was built, followed by the construction of a village to accommodate the multitude of workmen required for the project. The village included a school, hospital, mission hall and a licensed club.

The houses of Nantgwyllt and Cwm Elan, both of which have associations with the poet Shelley, were among the dwellings submerged by the reservoirs. It is said that Nantgwyllt was the subject of Francis Brett Young's novel 'The House Under the Water', and its garden walls can still be seen when Caban-coch's water levels are low. A church, chapel, school and numerous farms were submerged when the scheme was completed in 1904. It was inaugurated by King Edward VII.

The Claerwen Scheme was postponed until after the Second World War. In the original scheme it had been decided to build three reservoirs (the unfinished Dolymynach Dam was to have contained the lowest) but the new scheme made provision for only one – the Claerwen with a huge capacity of over 10,000 million gallons. It was completed in 1952 and inaugurated by Queen Elizabeth II and the Duke of Edinburgh.

through an avenue of larch and spruce to the metalled reservoir road, which it crosses in order to reach the lakeshore path that used to form a bed for the track of the constructors' railway (the imprints left by the wooden sleepers are still evident in places today). Although this track is beautiful and leads to the Carreg-ddu Dam and causeway just two miles by road from Elan Village, the superior route leaves it at 914657. Here a stream can be seen tumbling down on a rocky course south of Graig Dolfaenog before feeding the lake. The narrow path rises up the heather slopes before crossing the stream and reaching the grassy ridge south of Y Glog Fawr. On the south-western horizon the pale moorlands rise to a curious flat-topped hill with prominent twin cairns. This two-thousand

The view south across Penygarreg Reservoir to its dam and Graig Dolfaenog

footer is Drygarn Fawr, one of the highlights of tomorrow's itinerary.

Elan Village

The path veers north-eastwards and descends on a wide track well-used by motorcycles. In the view ahead the beautiful valleys of the Elan and the Wye are visible in a landscape that is softer and more fertile than any seen since Machynlleth. A brook is crossed and the way is lined with hawthorn, oak, silver birch and bracken. It then enters a small copse before passing by the ruined farmhouse to reach a lane. A cart track leaves the lane at 939665 and descends to the B4518 a couple of hundred yards east of the Elan Valley Hotel and about two miles from the charming small market town of Rhayader, whose fine inns can offer good food and wine.

The submerged Caban-coch dam topped by its road bridge

By the Carreg-ddu Reservoir on the course of the old railway

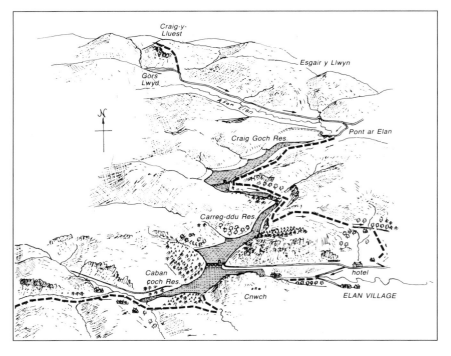

CHAPTER 8

ABERGWESYN AND THE TYWI
ELAN VILLAGE TO RHANDIRMYN

Unrivalled for aesthetic appeal, this section is characterised by its superb wild valleys and rushing streams, and the sheer variety of its scenery.

Elan's charms are manifested for the last time in fine elevated views from the slopes of Gro Hill. The route returns to the high lonely Elenydd Mountains on a path that twists through the rugged Rhiwnant Valley to its zenith on Drygarn Fawr, a high eminence whose craggy top is endowed with two huge beehive cairns, visible for many a mile.

After descending by the Irfon or Gwesyn valleys to the tiny hamlet of Abergwesyn the way ahead is on empty moorland to Llyn Brianne, a much newer reservoir than its Elan neighbours. With steep conifer-clad slopes surrounding its sinuous shorelines, Brianne lends to this corner of Wales a Norwegian fjord-like character. South of the 300ft dam the Tywi resumes its natural course, flowing boisterously through a group of little known hills whose splendour and alpine character far outweigh their modest proportions. The area is a haven for buzzards, redstarts, raven, pied flycatchers and a rare bird of prey, the red kite.

Two possible routes are offered through these hills. The shorter and less demanding encircles the rocky oak-covered peak of Dinas and follows the turbulent Afon Tywi, passing close to its impressive confluence with the Doethie, whose lower reaches are explored more intimately by a second route. This route has previously crossed the dam and traced Brianne's south-western shore before descending to Troed-rhiw-ruddwen.

The Tywi is pacified as its valley widens and it is almost subdued when meandering amongst the sleepy pastures of Rhandirmwyn and its outlying hamlet, Nant-y-Bai. Here in ideal riverside settings are three campsites served by two delightful country pubs. The Towey Bridge Inn and The Royal Oak.

The Caban-coch Reservoir
At Elan village the river flows over a stony bed beneath the oakwoods and crags of Cnwch. Towering above the river, the Caban-coch Dam is an alien giant, especially impressive when the reservoir's headwaters spill over its stone ramparts.

The route crosses the Elan at 931648 on a white suspension bridge and continues along a track leading south-westward through the woods. After about fifty yards the track is left for one that zig-zags up the slopes to reach a metalled lane terminating at the dam's edge.

The path now follows the bouldered shoreline of the reservoir before climbing the slopes of Cnwch alongside the

On the ascent of Gro Hill with the Caban-coch Reservoir in the background

forest of larches that cloaks Gro Hill. These two hills are divided by the Nant y Gro which flows from the wet grassy slopes of Y Gamriw. Retrospective views from Cnwch's slopes include a magnificent vista across the Caban-coch Reservoir, with its dam and causeway dividing it from the Carreg-ddu lake.

Gro Hill
Beyond the forest the edges of a really wild area are entered. The lower slopes of Y Gamriw are boulder-strewn and bracken-covered, decorated with isolated, dwarfed trees. A single stand of pine borders an old ruined cottage (927632) which is passed before the path veers south-west. After fording the Nant y Gro, the route rejoins the forest's edge to the north of Gro Hill where a wide,

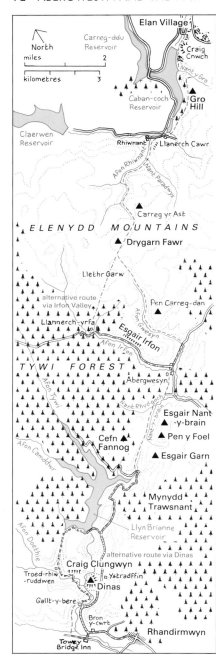

A retrospective view down the Rhiwnant Valley from above the mine workings on the route to Drygarn Fawr

short-grassed track descends luxuriously and delightfully to Llanerch Cawr farm which is situated at the south-western extremity of the Elan Valley reservoirs.

Rhiwnant Valley
Beyond Llanerch the route enters the valley of the Claerwen. After following a metalled road on the river's southern banks for about fifty yards, a farm track leads from a gate on the left-hand side to the Rhiwnant's lovely twisting valley, memorable for its wild solitude and serenity. The scene is at its most magnificent outside the summer months when, on a sunny day, the withered brackens are transformed into a flame-red mantle to the hills that flank the bustling river. A small stand of pine trees

complements the ruggedness of the surrounding landscape – a far cry from the endless conifer regiments of nearby plantations.

The farm road is left where it veers

One of the two huge summit cairns of Drygarn Fawr

southward alongside the Nant Para-dwys. After fording this stream near its confluence with the Rhiwnant our less obvious route continues up the south side of the Rhiwnant valley. The increasingly lively Rhiwnant's left banks are followed past some derelict mine workings. The winding valley narrows as it rises through the now more craggy and rough slopes of Drygarn Fawr where the path degenerates into a sheep track.

Drygarn Fawr

The Rhiwnant's banks are left at 873598, where a stream flowing from the ridge between Drygarn Fawr and Carreg yr Ast is followed to its source near the crags that mark the position of the latter peak. From here turn right taking a south-westerly course for Drygarn's two huge beehive cairns which crown the highest summit between Pumlumon and the Brecon Beacon/Carmarthen Fan escarpment to the south. These massifs are easily recognisable on a mist-free day in an expansive and interesting, if un-spectacular, panorama enlivened by views of the upper recesses of the Elan Valley reservoirs.

The Gwesyn Valley

A south-westerly route from Drygarn Fawr will lead to the upper valley of the Afon Gwesyn, whose course is followed until it meets the Irfon at Abergwesyn. This route is arduous in its upper reaches, the sometimes wettish ground being covered in thick tussocky grass but, as the valley deepens, a well-trodden path develops, leading the walker into a beautiful twisting gorge, two miles in length. Many broad-leafed trees decorate the bracken-clad stony slopes whilst the river itself is lined with wind-bent hawthorn. A newly built farm track is encountered which leads to Trysgol. From here the path descends the ensuing steep, wooded valley and on leaving the woods crosses a field, joining a rutted cart track near to the Gwesyn,

Looking back north up the Gwesyn Valley during the descent from Drygarn Fawr

Drygarn Fawr from the south

The tiny hamlet of Abergwesyn

Llyn Brianne – the reservoir that captures the upper waters of the Afon Tywi.

which it fords a little further down river.

Abergwesyn

The track meets a tarmac farm road and a left turn here will lead to the Beulah–Abergwesyn road by the tiny Post Office/General Store.

The route continues along the west-bound road which crosses the River Irfon at Abergwesyn. The main valley is left by a forestry road at the far side of the bridge which winds steeply up the hillside before entering the southern edge of the vast Tywi plantations, which blanket some 30 square miles of hills stretching northwards to Strata Florida. The forestry road is quit just prior to its entry into the plantations and the new path, from its left-hand side, leads down to the Llwyn-derw Hotel from where it continues along the featureless, grassy valley of the Nant-y-brain. This area has recently been the subject of great controversy. The Forestry Commission wanted to extend their Tywi plantations but were eventually defeated after a strong campaign by the Ramblers' Association. After the crossing of Nant Rhyd–goch, be careful not to be lured on to the wrong path which zig-zags up Cefn Fannog and goes westwards into the forest. A better path, avoiding the forests, stays close to the Nant-y-brain until that stream veers southwards around the skirts of Pen y Foel.

Llyn Brianne

The route maintains its south-westerly direction to the top of the pass north of Esgair Garn and thence descends to a road which contours around one of the scruffier fingers of the Llyn Brianne Reservoir.

Llyn Brianne, completed in 1972, holds 13,400,000 gallons of water to ensure an adequate supply to the Swansea area. Its sprawl is more obvious from further along the road to the south-west,

The stone-fill Brianne Dam with its dramatic waterspout outflow that maintains and aerates the Tywi

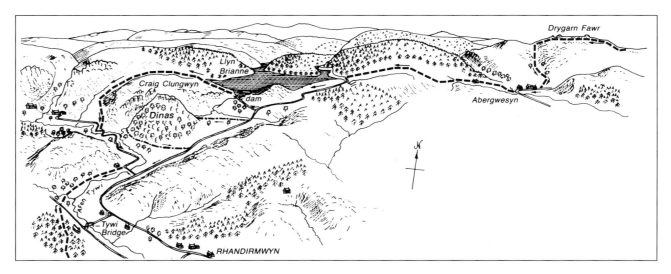

The spurs of the upper Doethie Valley (above) and the path alongside the Afon Doethie below Craig Clungwyn (left)

At the confluence of the Doethie and the Tywi between Craig Clungwyn and Dinas

from where the spruce-lined flooded valleys of the Camdwr and Tywi seem to recede like serpents to the barren Elenydd skyline.

At Bwlch-y-fin (794482 not marked on the 1:50,000 map), which is at the head of a verdant, fertile vale, a road to the right is taken and the lake's massive stone-fill dam and outfall are seen. To the left the Tywi resumes its course in a fine, rugged V-shaped valley. Our route continues over the dam and then follows a forestry road around the lake to its western extremity. Here another forestry road heads south-west, descending to Troed-rhiw-ruddwen in the beautiful Doethie Valley. As the farm is passed, the stark cliffs of Craig Pysgotwr appear above the lush pastures that surround the tree-lined Doethie river.

The path joins a narrow tarmac lane as the river turns ninety degrees beneath Craig Clungwyn, revealing a scene of bracken and a myriad oaks clothing the hillsides: a wonderful autumn sight. We are now in the midst of RSPB areas and a look to the skies could well reveal the rare red kite, regularly seen in this vicinity.

Tywi Valley

The lane follows the western banks of the Doethie until, in one of this walk's finest scenes, the powerful foaming torrents of the Tywi force their way through a narrow bouldered gorge between the Dinas and Craig Clungwyn (on 1:50,000). A rock outcrop hereabouts gives a fine platform from which to view this cataract and its confluence with the lively, if more subdued, Afon Doethie.

Half a mile further, the lane crosses the Tywi to meet the road from Llyn Brianne but it is forsaken for a track which follows the west side of the valley passing Gallt-y-bere farm and camping

Afon Tywi from the Llyn Brianne road showing Craig Clungwyn in the background and Dinas on the right

Looking west down the Tywi valley

The Towey Bridge Inn

Views of the Irfon Valley near Abergwesyn: the northerly aspect with Esgair Irfon on the right (above)

Looking south to the Afon Irfon with the Tywi Forest on the skyline

Llannerch-yrfa at the head of the Irfon valley

site. The Tywi is below and to the south flowing on a wide bed through green pastures. As the river turns southwards a very narrow country lane is encountered which descends steeply, crosses a tributary of the Tywi and ascends just as steeply to meet another lane. A left turn here will lead to the Towey Bridge Inn, a whitewashed building near the riverbank and opposite a steel bridge. A backdrop of spruce and larch on the hillside which rises from the back garden, and the smattering of colour provided by the owner's peacocks, complete a charming rural scene.

There is a campsite at Bron-y-cwrt farm (across the bridge in the fields to the right) but for those requiring more luxury the Royal Oak at Rhandirmwyn, one and a half miles down river, though a little off-route, is highly recommended.

ROUTE VARIATIONS

Drygarn Fawr to Abergwesyn
via the Irfon Valley

From the summit of Drygarn Fawr take a south-westerly course over Llethr Garw before entering a forest (unmarked on some 1:50,000 maps) via a small gate. A grassy firebreak marks the right of way which descends a spur between the Nant y Fedw and an unnamed stream. To follow the bridleway you will have to ignore the zig-zags of the forestry roads and maintain direction, but the way becomes briefly indistinct after crossing another un-named stream. It is easier in this case to utilise the Commission's roads which join the Irfon Valley and Tregaron mountain road by the stone cottage, Llannerchyrfa, sited amidst a welcome oasis of broad-leafed trees. The Nant y Fedw ripples, shallow and clear, over a golden pebble bed by the farm's side to join forces with the larger river.

The mountain road is followed to Abergwesyn two and a half miles south, its course leading the traveller through one of Wales' wildest and most delightful valleys, the Irfon. The bare ragged crags of the upper region give way to dense oakwoods that form part of a nature reserve (Nant Irfon) frequented by many species of bird including buzzards, pied flycatchers and kite.

Llyn Brianne to Rhandirmwyn
via Dinas

This takes the Brianne–Rhandirmwyn lane in favour of the more intricate main route. It includes a circuit through the nature reserve and provides a beautiful alternative way which should not be lightly dismissed, especially if limbs are tiring or time is short. The path around Dinas starts by the chapel at Ystradffin, passes over wetlands to reach the banks of the Afon Tywi as it squeezes between the crowding flanks of Dinas and Craig Clungwyn, then threads its way through the oakwoods, around rocks, past nesting boxes until it once again reaches the Rhandirmwyn lane. One and a half miles on it passes Bron-y-cwrt farm near to the Towey Bridge Inn, thus rejoining the main route.

The Afon Tywi where it flows through the gorge between Dinas and Craig Clungwyn

Looking east along the Carmarthen Fan escarpment to Bannau Sir Gaer

CHAPTER 9

THE BARRIER: CARMARTHEN FAN
RHANDIRMWYN TO CRAIG-Y-NOS

Laid before us is another day of beautiful countryside culminating in the ascent of Carmarthen Fan, whose distinctive profiles, carved from red sandstone, have been eagerly anticipated since their first sighting from Pumlumon.

Rather than follow lanes from Rhandirmwyn to Llandovery, two rather devious hill routes are offered which are preferable in that they open up views invisible from the valley floor. One involves retracing steps to Nant-y-Bai and ascending the slopes of Mynydd Mallaen. A second route follows the Tywi's banks for a mile before climbing to the eastern side of the green hills of the Fforest Ridge before descending a quiet country lane to Llandovery.

More country lanes are used in the approach to Carmarthen Fan. The main route continues on high moorland tracks to the Usk Reservoir whose immediate surroundings are somewhat marred by conifer plantations.

On the final approaches to Fan Foel sudden changes unfold and moorland becomes mountain. The smooth grassy slopes give way in the north and west to eroded tawny cliffs, layered with gritstone strata and broken by tight cwms. From the top a superb ridge walk along firm quartzite beds leads to Bannau Brycheiniog, the highest peak in South-West Wales, which commands extensive views. The Brecon Beacons, Black Mountains and Pumlumon all arouse interest in vast panoramas on clear days.

When the clouds hang low on the hills this route is not easily navigated in the region of the Usk Reservoir and the alternative route via the hamlet of Llanddeusant is preferable. It uses a Water Board track to Llyn y Fan fach which is cradled by the cliffs of Bannau Sir Gaer. The escarpment's northern edge is then followed to Bannau Brycheiniog where the Usk Reservoir approach is joined. Both routes use the magnificent long descent along the slender ridge of Fan Hir which leads directly to the Tawe Valley and almost to the front door of the Tafarn-y-Garreg Inn.

It must be added that, in all except the summer months, this section of the route is perhaps the hardest to complete in one day. In poor weather conditions or when there are limited hours of daylight, it will be necessary to make a realistic assessment about whether or not there is enough time or energy to cross Carmarthen Fan at the end of the day.

Nant-y-Bai

From Rhandirmwyn it will be tempting to follow the attractive leafy lanes that lead to Llandovery. However a far finer route traverses the eastern slope of Mynydd Mallaen where the views reveal so much more of the beautiful scenery than those from the valley itself where the lanes are densely hedged.

The forestry road that is used to climb the slopes of Mynydd Mallaen is four hundred yards along the Dolaucothi road from the Towey Bridge Inn. As it leaves the lower plantations, the restricted views are transformed to airy scenes

On Mynydd Mallaen above the Tywi Valley

of the Tywi Valley around Nant-y-Bai, where the distant white cottages seem to be huddled for shelter at the foot of Cnwch, a small rounded hill separated from the northern hillsides by the Nant-y-Bai stream. Beyond Cnwch, the grey spoil heaps of a disused lead-mine, now surrounded by vast young conifer plantations, are a reminder of what was once a flourishing industry in these parts.

Cwm-y-Rhaiadr

Near to the plantation's exit at Cwm-saethe an old track branches to the left of the forestry road. This in turn leads to a gate (767442) at the edge of a high

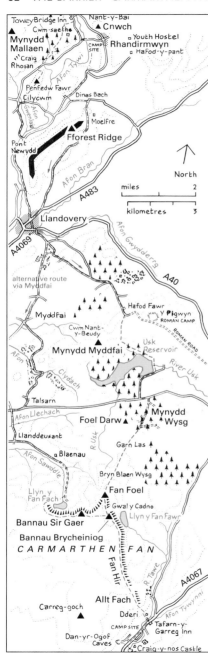

The view west across the Tywi Valley to Mynydd Mallaen from near Rhandirmwyn

meadow across which the Brecon Beacons and Carmarthen Fan can be seen on the horizon.

After maintaining a south-south-westerly direction over the meadow the Cwm Rhaiadr Plantations are entered and a narrow descending path is followed through the dark woods until it meets a wide forestry track at an acute angle. Glimpses of high waterfalls cascading from the Craig Ddu cliffs can be seen through gaps in the stands of spruce.

The forestry road to be used leads south-westwards before switching back to a junction (764427) where a right turn is taken. After turning left at the next junction and following the road southwards for a short while a leafy path on its right-hand side descends to the Nant y Rhaeadr which it crosses via a wooden footbridge. The path then ascends to a cart track meeting a country lane at 762422 opposite a small terrace of cottages.

Three hundred yards southwards along the lane, a farm track on the left

passes through a small forest. It ends at a farmhouse but a path to the west of it goes to the top of a hill, Penfedw Fawr, which stands alone between the merging valleys of Tywi and Gwenlais, provid-

The main square of Llandovery

ing an excellent vantage point. The northern and western prospects are dominated by Mynydd Mallaen whose expansive slopes are severed by the deep gorges cut by the Gwenlais and its tributary, the Merchon, whilst another of its streams tumbles down the rocky cwm by Craig Rhosan creating what is, after a period of rainfall, a magnificent waterfall. To the south is the village of Cilycwm, quiet in its pastures and surrounded on three sides by gentle, green rolling hills – so different from the wild Elenydd landscapes of the previous day. The path descends by the eastern boundaries of a small conifer forest and across fields to the village. A building worth noting here is the fifteenth century church of St Michael, secluded from the main street with its guttering of cobbles by fine, dark, mature yew trees.

Cilycwm to Llandovery

Although there is a footpath along the eastern banks of the Gwenlais to Pont Newydd it is quicker and better to travel along the twisting country lanes to the same spot. Here the Tywi is crossed and a right turn and a three-mile road walk lead to Llandovery, a place which that famous traveller of a century ago, George Borrow, described as 'The pleasantest little town in which I have halted in the course of my wanderings'.

Alternative route from Rhandirmwyn to Llandovery via Fforest Ridge

This route is more direct than the itinerary through Cilycwm and will suit those who are looking for a quicker way to Llandovery so as to leave more time for Carmarthen Fan. It begins by heading south along the banks of the Tywi from the Camping Club entrance (778436) through a complex of fields and copses.

Shortly after fording a streamlet on stepping stones the path veers from the riverbank following the direction of a stand of trees and then a wire fence. Beyond a small stile a bracken-lined track then ascends through scrubland to the foot of a wooded hill (not named on the 1:50,000 map). A metal five-bar gate

is used as an entry to a field whose left-hand corner is to be reached before turning right (south-east) on an obvious track through woodland to reach a country lane at 781422.

The lane is followed to Dinas Bach, a mile to the south, where a path crosses south-eastwards across a field. It reaches a very narrow lane, which half a mile to the east is left for a farm road marked 'Moelfre'. The tarmac lane becomes a gated dirt track and views of the wide green valley of the Afon Bran are lovely, as is the pleasant little wooded dell fronting Moelfre farm. The road heads south to a fork (785395) where a delightful winding lane heads south-west down attractive hill slopes high above Llandovery, revealing panoramas of the meandering Afon Bran and the tree-clad heights further distant. As it descends, the hedges obscure the scenery beyond, although glimpses may be had through the occasional farm gates. The narrow

Tywi Gorge near Rhandirmwyn

A view up the Tywi Valley from the hills west of Llandovery – Fforest Ridge is on the right

lane meets the busy A483 half a mile north-east of Llandovery.

Llandovery

Llandovery is known in Welsh as Llanymyddfri – 'the church amongst the waters'. It was once occupied by the Romans whose fort, Alabum, was sited near to St Mary's church by the Afon Bran to the north of the town.

The castle, built for the Norman baron Richard Fitz Pons in the twelfth century, was captured by the Welsh in the Glyndwr Revolts. In 1532 its owner Rhys-ap-Gruffydd was executed at the hands of Henry VIII for treason and, in an act of revenge by the Welsh, the castle was destroyed never to be rebuilt.

The town's history is intertwined with the fortunes of the cattle drovers who were so important in the rural communities before the railway age. When thieves made travelling on Wales's lonely and rugged roads a hazardous exercise, the local farmers hired them to drive cattle to the more lucrative markets of England and to settle for them accounts with non-local people. This

meant that drovers needed to handle large sums of money and led to the introduction of banking systems – some of them even issuing bank notes. One of the most successful of these was David Jones' 'Black Ox Bank' which eventually had offices in Llandovery, Llandeilo and Tregaron before being taken over at the turn of the twentieth century by Lloyds Bank. Modern day Llandovery has two cafes and numerous public houses to replenish the needs of body and soul, and it may be with regret that it is left on the Brecon-bound A40. Before leaving the town a right turn along the lane signposted 'Myddfai' leads across the Afon Gwydderig at the Waterloo Bridge and, after maintaining direction at the crossroads (776339), the winding lane ascends the rolling hilly country amongst sylvan landscapes.

Mynydd Myddfai

After a walk of about three miles the road divides at 811320 at a signpost 'To Halfway' and the route takes the right fork – a metalled cul-de-sac passing by Hafod Fawr farm. This is part of the old

Looking south across the Usk Reservoir to Carmarthen Fan

Bannau Sir Gaer and Llyn y Fan fach from Fan Foel

Roman Road between Llandovery and Brecon and, as can be seen on the map, it passes many Roman relics, the most impressive being the old marching camp, Y Pigwyn. A couple of hundred yards south of the farm the road which deteriorates into a rutted track, is left for a grassy track heading south-south-west initially through heather, matted grass and profuse bracken, and then climbing the rugged, bare northern slopes of Mynydd Myddfai reaching open fellside beyond a five-bar gate. Retrospective views across the undulating upland pastures include the oakwoods of the nearby Halfway Forest and further afield beyond the Tywi Valley the hills of Central Wales, notably Drygarn Fawr. On the southern horizon, past the dark spruce mantle surrounding the still obscured Usk Reservoir and the pale ochre moorlands to its south, the sandstone escarpment of Carmarthen Fan rises high.

Usk Reservoir

The indistinct bridleway over the summit of Mynydd Myddfai meets the ancient 'green road' from Cwm Nant-y-Beudy. As this is followed towards the spruce woods to the south the far shores of the Usk Reservoir are at last revealed. A wooden gate (818297) marks the entry to the forest and a path continues on a Commission road descending to the lakeshore.

After turning left (east-south-east) on a tarmac road, the reservoir's earth-fill dam, which spans 1,400ft and holds back 2000 million gallons of water, is crossed to reach another lane which is followed through more forest to its junction with the Trecastle-Talsarn road at 828274. After turning left towards Trecastle a forestry track leading southwards from 833275 is followed over Mynydd Wysg (Welsh spelling of Usk and pronounced the same) to the plantation's southern exit (832262) and the relief of open land to the east of Foel Darw.

Ahead lie the dominant cliffs of Fan Foel and Bannau Brycheiniog, Carmarthen Fan's highest peaks, and the spirit is rejuvenated at the prospect of some more high mountains, the first since Pumlumon.

There is a slight descent south of Foel Darw and the mountains temporarily disappear from view, but reappear on the ascent of the vast moorland slopes of Garn Las. If conditions are unsuitable for a high mountain traverse a detour could be made from here following a right of way eastwards past Blaenau Uchaf and Isaf farms to reach a country lane at 846257. The lane in turn leads to the Black Mountain Road which crosses barren moorlands to reach the Tawe valley.

The tracks on Garn Las are sketchy and would be difficult to locate in mist. A south-westerly course leads to the spur of Bryn Blaen Wysg (not named on 1:50,000 maps) where the source of the River Usk (Afon Wysg) can be seen (819238).

Fan Foel

The path rises more steeply from the foot to the summit of Fan Foel but the surroundings are memorable and dramatic, far removed from the preceding barren moors.

To the west, the angular escarpment of Bannau Sir Gaer displays its abrupt northern facade to Llyn y Fan fach below. The horizontal strata of the rust-coloured old red sandstone and grey millstone grit are typical of South Wales' Great Escarpment which comprises The Black Mountains, Brecon Beacons, Fforest Fawr and Carmarthen Fan, but the contrast between these landscapes and the more conventional mountain scenery of previous days in the north of the principality is unexpected. Ahead is the cwm known as Gwal y Cadno

Bannau Brycheiniog from the slopes of Fan Hir above Bwlch Giedd

between Fan Foel and Bannau Brycheiniog (not marked on 1:50,000 maps) with vertical walls of red sandstone, whilst to the north the Usk Reservoir, cradled in its nest of dark green spruces, dominates the sparse moorland vista.

Bannau Brycheiniog

From the summit of Fan Foel to that of Bannau Brycheiniog is half a mile of easy and pleasant ridge walking. The path keeps to the edge of the range's steep eastern ramparts and a second lake, Llyn y Fan fawr is seen a few hundred feet below. The twin peaks of the Brecon Beacons should be easily spotted on the eastern horizon.

There is a three hundred foot drop to Bwlch Giedd before the ascent of the narrow ridge of Fan Hir, whose broken gritstone crags fall steeply to high, lonely moorland to its east. Across the lonely valleys of the Tawe and the

Tywynni the graceful lines of Fan Gyhirych arrest the attention. From this viewpoint the 2,300ft peak bears a strong resemblance to Tyrrau Mawr in the Cadair Idris range.

From Fan Hir there is a glorious easy-paced descent southwards along the ridge to the Tawe valley over Allt Fach,

Looking south along the Fan Hir ridge

Carmarthen Fan from a lane near Llanddeusant

THE LADY OF THE LAKE AND THE PHYSICIANS OF MYDDFAI

Rhiwallon, who was a son of the farmer of Blaensawdde farm, near Llanddeusant, was tending cattle near Llyn y Fan fach when he saw a beautiful young maiden. He instantly fell in love with the girl, who was sitting by the lakeshore combing her long hair, and, offering her bread that his mother had prepared for his lunch, he asked her to marry him. She refused, saying that the bread was too hard and she vanished into the depths of the lake.

On the next day he brought a different type of bread but still it did not meet with her approval. On the third meeting his offering of unleavened bread was found acceptable and the girl agreed to marry him but attached one condition. She told him that she was not an ordinary mortal and that she would return to her kind if he struck her three times. Rhiwallon accepted her condition and they were happily married with three sons. The inevitable happened. It is said that the third time he struck her was after she had giggled at a funeral, and although it was hardly more than a tap, the lady of the lake disappeared from his life as mysteriously as she had first appeared.

The three sons however searched for her, and their efforts were rewarded when she appeared from the waters of Llyn y Fan fach. She taught them about medicine and cures for the sick, showing them useful herbs from the mountainsides. The three boys became the first in a long line of 'Physicians of Myddfai'. Many local doctors claim that they are related, the last being Dr. C. Rice Williams of Aberystwyth, who died in 1842.

the southern outpost (not marked on 1:50,000 maps).

From Allt Fach the greenness of the Tawe valley below is very evident, as are the brilliant white walls of Dderi farmhouse. The path down the hillside is very steep and passes on the north side of some farm buildings (848174) before veering left alongside the banks of a clear, cool chattering stream; just the place to rest a while and dip your feet.

Glyntawe

The Tawe is crossed on a fine new footbridge (848173) and the route then follows a track which terminates at the A4067 opposite the Tafarn-y-Garreg public house at Glyntawe, the verdant head of the beautiful Upper Swansea Valley. The sandstone mountain architecture has changed to one of limestone, evident in the ramparts of the shapely peak of Cribarth which stands at a bend in the valley one and a half miles to the south. Between Tafarn-y-Garreg and Cribarth are the limestone caves at Dan-

yr-Ogof which are renowned for their fine floodlit chambers displaying some fine stalagmite and stalactite formations.

Bannau Sir Gaer from the Water Board filter beds below Llyn y Fan fach

They are highly recommended for those who can spare the time. The Dan-yr-Ogof complex also includes a good

motel, and a campsite nicely set amongst trees and fairly close to both the Tafarn-y-Garreg and the Gwyn Arms.

Alternative route to Carmarthen Fan from Llandovery via Myddfai

The moorlands surrounding the Usk Reservoir and to the north of Carmarthen Fan can be awkward to navigate in mist due to their lack of features. A route passing through the village of Myddfai and the Sawdde Valley on its way to the peak is a much more viable alternative when such conditions prevail.

The eight miles of country lanes between Llandovery and Llanddeusant are a joy to walk. Few cars will be seen on a journey which veers from the main route at the crossroads (776339) where it pursues a southbound course to Myddfai. Here there is a pub, a few houses and a picturesque small church whose elevated churchyard is decorated with daffodils. It is possible to use either of two routes from the village to Llanddeusant but the one that leads south-eastwards to the foot of Mynydd Myddfai is the more picturesque and is especially beautiful in the region of the Afon Clydach.

In Llanddeusant, Talsarn and the Cross Inn are passed before a south-bound tree-lined lane descends deep into the valley of the Afon Llechach before rising tortuously to Llanddeusant. The hamlet's fine church dates back to the fourteenth century. There is also a Youth Hostel here which may provide a stopping place at the end of a short day from Rhandirmwyn.

Llyn y Fan fach

From Llanddeusant a narrow metalled track follows the northern flanks of the Sawdde Valley, whose rich emerald fields divided by thick hedgerows and scattered farmhouses contrast with the stark, bare hills of Carmarthen Fan which rise to their south.

Beyond Blaenau farm, a Water Board track rises on the east banks of the Sawddle to its source, Llyn y Fan fach. Behind the small lake tower the crags, Ba'r y Llyn (unmarked on 1:50,000 map),

On the ascent to Tyle Gwyn with Llyn y Fan fach and Bannau Sir Gaer in the background

whose visible grit and sandstone strata are strangely gnarled and faulted.

Bannau Sir Gaer

A path rises from the north shores of the lake westwards on a grassy spur to reach the ridge at Tyle Gwyn. From here are inspiring views across Llyn y Fan fach to the angular profile of Bannau Sir Gaer, and further afield, Fan Foel. The cliff edges are followed to Bannau Sir Gaer's summit and then to the pass beneath Fan Foel where an easterly course is taken on rough trackless ground to the summit of Bannau Brycheiniog and joins the main route.

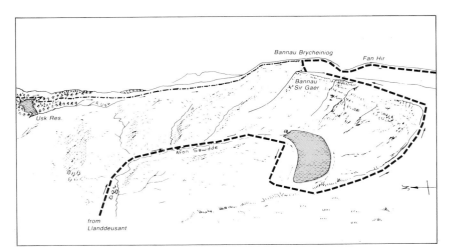

Looking back up the Fan Hir ridge on the descent to Glyntawe

The view north-east from Cribarth to Carmarthen Fan (Bannau Brycheiniog and Fan Hir) and Fan Gihirych

CHAPTER 10

BLACK MOUNTAIN
CRAIG-Y-NOS TO THE AMAN VALLEY

The penultimate leg of the walk commences with a splendid peak, Cribarth, whose limestone architecture has all the hallmarks of greater eminences.

After the traverse of this fine little peak the succeeding tracks and country lanes wend their way through pastures and traverse industrial valleys whose cultures are synonymous with South Wales. Even amongst these conurbations there are moorland peaks wild enough to give a false impression of remoteness. This is very evident in such hills as Mynydd y Gwair in the Lliw Valley or Bryn Mawr, which are both less than a mile from the road. This urban route provides the most direct approach to the Gower and the end of our walk. However, for those who yearn for one more day in the mountains there is an alternative high-level route crossing the Black Mountain range (not to be confused with the mountains east of the Brecon Beacons) from east to west and giving seventeen miles of high, trackless mountain terrain which will provide a very stiff navigational exercise in poor conditions.

On this section of the walk we get the first real views of the South Wales coastline and even a harbinger of the final promenade along the Gower coast.

Craig-y-nos Castle

In comparison with the lofty heights of Carmarthen Fan, Cribarth's elevation of 1,388ft seems pretty humble, but when seen from the floor of the Tawe Valley it is obvious that this shapely little limestone peak has a great deal of character.

Standing at the foot of the mountain in a setting of woodland and beautiful garden is the ornate, Gothic-styled Craig-y-nos Castle. It was bought in 1879 by Adelina Patti, the famous Spanish opera singer who found it an ideal secluded retreat into which she and her lover, the tenor Ernest Nicolini, could retire. She extended the castle to include a theatre which is still used today. On her death in 1919 Craig-y-nos was donated to the community and converted to a hospital which was named in her memory. Recently this has been closed and there is doubt as to the future of the building, although a preservation order has been placed to protect the theatre.

Cribarth

Opposite the castle and next to Pentre Cribarth Farm and Equestrian Centre, a signposted footpath leads westwards across a field and thence climbs the hill's northern slopes on an eroded red sand-

Craig-y-nos Castle

stone-surfaced track above a line of hawthorn and rowan trees. In retrospective views there is much to admire. The irregular tree-lined pastures of the Tawe valley rise to the gentle lower slopes of the surrounding mountainsides of Fan Hir and Fan Gihirych. The grey snaking highway does nothing to depreciate the scene and the muffled sounds from busy traffic only add to the quiet calm of the hill.

The path veers southwards, ascends to the pale limestone crags and bluffs of Cribarth's north-eastern buttress, and then follows a grassy track on the southern flank of the summit plateau bounded on one side by a stone wall and on the other by fine crags. Alternatively the craggy summit ridge, disfigured in places by quarrying, allows views to the north. The summit, situated at the western end of the plateau and distinguished by a concrete trig point, offers a fine platform from which to view the lower Swansea Valley and the industrial towns of Ystalyfera, Ystradgynlais and Pontardawe. Beyond these hills, if clear conditions allow, the coastline around Swansea Bay can be distinguished whilst in northern prospects, across the wild

Cribarth from the upper Swansea valley near Glyntawe

stony wastelands of Carreg-goch, lie the Carmarthen Fan summits of Bannau Brycheiniog and Fan Hir.

It is on Cribarth's summit that the decision must be made whether to follow the high-level traverse of the lonely limestone Black Mountain peaks or to take the much less strenuous low route across a strange mixture of agricultural and industrial lands.

To the south and west of the summit are limestone quarries and a complex of old tramways. One such tramway, which terminates at a bluff adjacent to the summit, is utilised by the low-level route for the descent along the crest of a grassy western spur (ignore the obvious track which leads to Abercraf).

The Giedd Forest

One mile west of Cribarth's summit the path descends the spur's northern grassy flanks to the Giedd Forest. A track which follows the edge of the conifer plantation enters deciduous woodland before reaching the large farm of Neuadd-lwyd, where a metalled lane leads south along the sylvan valley of the Afon Giedd. At 787118 after a left turn at a junction, the Giedd is crossed on a small bridge. The path that follows ascends some wooded slopes in a series of flag-stone steps before crossing two fields whose boundaries are crossed using kissing gates to reach a country lane at 780118. This winds through farming country to the south of opencast coal workings and passes close to a trig point strangely situated in a meadow.

Cwmtwrch uchaf

The lane is left at 774111 when a track leading westwards past a golf course is followed to its termination at an old farmhouse half a mile distant. An indistinct southerly course links the route with a rutted track which crosses lofty pastureland to reach another more dilapidated farm building. A descent is then made on a twisting lane to Cwmtwrch uchaf, an austere industrial valley town situated in a deep glen at the confluence of the Afon Twrch and Nant Gwys. If Craig-y-nos was left at breakfast time then it will probably be close to lunchtime and Cwmtwrch can offer two public houses and a few shops to serve this purpose before continuing the journey.

From the roadside at 757110 a path climbs south-west out of the Twrch Valley through delightful woodland offering impressive views of Garreg-lwyd and Foel Fraith, two Black Mountain peaks. A black-surfaced path leading from the exit of the woods to the lane which leads west to Rhiwfawr (Pen Rhiwfawr on pre 1985 maps) is a reminder that we are in coal-mining country.

Mynydd Uchaf

Rhiwfawr, a weatherbeaten high hillside village, is passed and the route follows the steep gradient of the Rhydyfro lane until 742108 when a cart track on its northern side ascends the grassy ridge of Mynydd Uchaf. As the trig point is reached superb northern panoramas of the Black Mountain and Carmarthen Fan are revealed across the scars of the opencast coalfields and towns of the Aman Valley. In contrasting southern views the rounded townside hills of Pontardawe, Neath and Swansea form an interesting pattern, their moderate elevations being tamed by the expanding

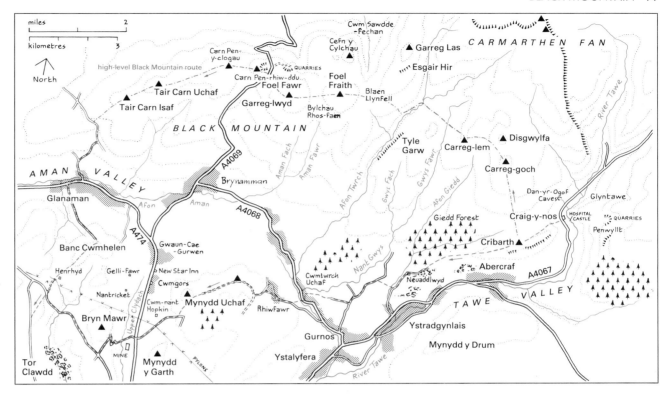

Looking north-west from Cwmtwrch towards the western end of the Black Mountain

needs of urban and forestry development.

On Mynydd Uchaf it is difficult to forget that we are in industrial Glamorgan, for its unkempt eastern slopes are littered with relics of our 'throw away' society – a rusty discarded fridge, the odd car tyre – signs that these hills are less cherished than their wild northern neighbours.

The Upper Clydach Valley

The cart track deteriorates and three closely grouped stone cairns are passed before a descent to a country lane at Cwm-nant Hopkin which leads down to the Upper Clydach Valley. Beyond a line of electricity pylons it enters more cultivated pastoral countryside with

COAL

Anthracite mining at Abernant and the Aman Valley

The once serene valleys of Glamorgan and Gwent were, in the nineteenth century, caught up in the rush to extract coal to fuel the burgeoning energy needs created by the Industrial Revolution. The new communities that developed around the mines were restricted by the narrowness of the valley floors, and their pit villages are characterised by the rows of slate-built terraced cottages lining the steep surrounding slopes. Because of the lack of room the slag and other waste products of the mine were transported and deposited on the mountains. Landslides caused by movement within the spoil heaps were not uncommon, culminating in 1967 with the terrible Aberfan disaster when a village school was buried, killing an entire generation of children.

Since the Second World War there has been a rapid decline in the Coal Industry caused by cheap imports from Europe and by nuclear power. The coalfields of Wales have been especially badly hit and the mines have closed one by one. The dark slag heaps have been flattened and landscaped and the hillsides cloaked by conifers.

Images of colliers' soot-darkened faces in dramas like 'How Green is my Valley' are brought to mind whenever Welsh industry is considered, and it is fitting that the walk passes through coal country as a reminder of this aspect of local culture. In this case it is the Aman and Clydach Valleys. Their product anthracite is a hard, black coal which has a very high (92%) carbon content and burns with a smokeless flame. The South Wales Coalfield is Western Europe's only source of the fuel and, as such, has little difficulty in finding suitable markets.

Abernant Colliery north of Pontardawe was completed in 1958 to mine the rich 'Red Vein' 1,200ft below the surface. The even deeper 'Peacock Vein' is said to consist of the finest anthracite in the world, but mining here is impossible due to the intense geological pressures at this depth.

Over 1,100 men are employed at Abernant, 950 at the pit and 160 at the neighbouring washery. Its annual production varies due to what the Coal Board describes as 'fickle geology', but is generally in the region of 200,000 tonnes per annum. Within its eight-square-mile take the mine contains 44 miles of underground roadways where more than 10 miles of high-speed belt-conveyors take coal from the Red Vein seams to the surface and then on to the washery. Here the coal is washed and graded, and then trans-ported by road or rail to its destination.

When completed in 1978 *The Betws Colliery* at Ammanford was the first mine to be constructed within Wales for ten years. Twin drifts (sloping tunnels) give access to the Red Vein which is mined here by a team of over 700 men who produce 375,000 tonnes per annum in one of Europe's most modern and efficient plants. In 1985 £15 million was spent on extensions, including a new drift and a wide-diameter venti-lation shaft drilled from the surface.

Opencast mining, which began after the Second World War, is still in operation in the Aman Valley at Garnant and near Bryn-amman. The method produces a very high quality anthracite which improves the mix of that mined from deeper sources. Huge earth moving machines are used to remove overlying earth above the shallow seams, which are then excavated before the top-soils are restored and the site landscaped.

Abernant Colliery

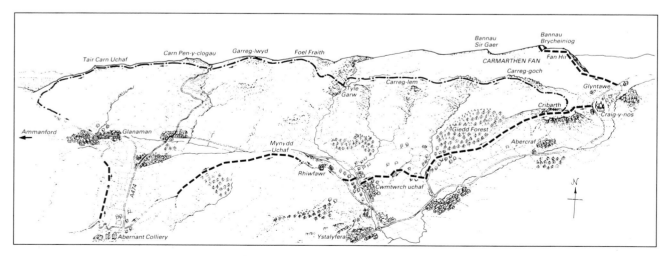

views down to the busy anthracite coal-mine of Abernant lying beneath the stark hills of Bryn Mawr and Mynydd y Gwair which rise on the valley's western side, though the trees that line the A474 do help to obscure the colliery workings.

The New Star Inn, a mile to the north at Cwmgors, offers accommodation to those who wish to retire for the day, but I feel that a slight detour northwards to the Aman Valley coal-mining towns would add to the richness and diversity of the route.

The A474 is crossed and the route continues along a lane signposted 'Baran' which skirts the north side of the colliery before zig-zagging up the steep sides of

Bryn Mawr. (Those wishing to press on to the Gower could follow the lane before turning right at the crossroads continuing to 670095, near Hendre farm, where the main route is joined. This route could also be utilised by those who stayed at the New Star Inn.) At the apex of the fourth bend (695087) a track leads northwards to a farm, Nant-y-gafaelau (not marked on 1:50,000 maps). From here it descends north-north-east across fields to Nant-melyn and thence to the farms of Nantricket and Gelli-fawr before reaching a country lane at 692116.

The Aman Valley

The views of the Black Mountain across industrial towns and mine workings become increasingly impressive on this section of the route. There is a real sense of the area's inherent Welshness on reaching Garnant in the bustling Aman Valley. Here the inhabitants are predominantly Welsh speaking (most street signs are written in both languages) but these are friendly people who will make your stay a welcome one. Their towns prospered on the riches of the hard, black anthracite coal resources which are still mined at Betws on the outskirts of Ammanford.

Ammanford, although a little off-route (3 miles) boasts many fine hotels and guest-houses for those who want a little extra comfort. It would be easy to regain the main route by using the country lane from Betws to the Lliw Hills near Penlle'r-castell (665097).

THE HIGH MOUNTAIN ALTERNATIVE

In clear conditions many walkers will favour the high-level alternative which traverses seventeen magnificent miles of remote, little-known limestone countryside to the north of the lower route.

Disgwylfa and Carreg-goch from Carreg-lem

Carreg-goch

From Cribarth's summit trig point the route descends northwards by bleached limestone terraces before a long ascent up the expansive stony flanks that rise to Carreg-goch. From this lofty vantage point the shapely Fan Gihirych can be seen across the boulder-strewn slopes. Further south are serrated cliffs formed by the vast quarries at Penwyllt high above the Swansea Valley. To the north and east views are restricted by the Carmarthen Fan tops – Bannau Brycheiniog and Fan Hir. Although their precipitous cliffs are hidden from view these fine hills dominate the scenery for much of the day.

Carreg-lem and the Twrch Crossing

A descent is made north-west across the flank of an equally craggy hill, Disgwylfa, where the slopes level off and veer west to Carreg-lem, crossing the depression formed by the Afon Giedd which flows beneath the surface hereabouts. Beyond Carreg-lem long, golden grasses indicate

a boggy area that feeds Gwys Fawr. This can be avoided by taking a north-westerly course to reach the best fording point on the Afon Twrch at 788187. The attention is now dominated by the immense grey craggy slopes of Esgair Hir which lead to the summit Gareg Las. These are best scaled from a little to the south-west, where the fast flowing Twrch is hemmed in, on the opposite bank, by the steep limestone-cragged slopes at the northern end of Tyle Garw.

The Afon Twrch when it is channelled by the Tyle Gawr defile

Garreg-lwyd from Carn Pen-rhiw-ddu looking over the dip where the A4069 crosses the Black Mountain massif

Foel Fraith

From the vicinity of 783183 climb the slopes heading west, passing to the south of a craggy area (not marked on the 1:50,000 map). This course leads directly to the pass, Blaen Llynfell, which sits between Gareg Las and the rounded grassy Foel Fraith which is easily recognised by its quarrying scars. Here amidst some boggy ground lie two small pools. To the north the graceful grassy flanks of Cefn y Cylchau fall to the deep hollow of Cwm Sawdde-Fechan, leading the eye to the beautiful rolling Carmarthenshire (Dyfed) hills beyond. The path ascending Foel Fraith circumvents numerous shakeholes (surface hollows formed by collapsing underground chambers) on its way to the plateau-like summit.

Garreg-lwyd

A descent of three hundred feet to Bylchau Rhos-faen precedes the short slog to the summit of Garreg-lwyd which at 2022ft is the highest top on this section of the walk. The summit is a distinctive place with huge stone shelters, and even the trig point is built from the thick layered limestone terrain. The views are interesting and include a new aspect of Carmarthen Fan with glimpses of the dark cliffs of Bannau Sir Gaer and Fan Foel at the zenith of rising moorland to the east. The view northwards across the more modest Carmarthenshire hills is now very expansive and impressive and it is possible with care to distinguish the peaks of Drygarn Fawr and Pumlumon on the horizon. In views to the south, industrial plains surrounding Brynamman and Gwaun-Cae-Gurwen lead the eye to the Upper Clydach Valley where the Abernant Colliery is sandwiched between the barren Lliw Hills and Mynydd y Garth.

Foel Fawr car-park

A north-westerly course across Garreg-lwyd's stony slopes leads down to the twisting A4067 at an altitude of 1618ft. On this high pass are the disused Foel Fawr quarries and a car-park.

The road is crossed and an ascent is made westwards on the southern slopes of Carn Pen-rhiw-ddu. Although it may seem logical from the map to aim for this summit and Carn Pen-y-clogau, this high line crosses ground that is rough and extremely marshy and it is better to take a parallel course across the southern slopes just above another marshy area on the lower slopes. The south-western section of the ridge is still rough in places, being thickly cloaked in heather with concealed boulders, but offers a much easier and drier passage.

Tair Carn Uchaf

After crossing a well-defined bridleway west of Carn Pen-y-clogau (713183) it is best to aim directly for the large cairns of Tair Carn Uchaf which are said to date back to the bronze age. The craggy peak commands superb views to the coast beyond the Aman and Loughor Valleys. However, the most arresting aspect is that to the north, where Carreg-Cennen Castle is seen perched precariously on vertical limestone cliffs. The castle, which was probably built in the twelfth century for Rhys-ap-Gruffydd, was captured by Owain Glyndwr in his struggles **against the English**. After the Wars of **the Roses** it was overrun by bandits who **terrorised** the neighbourhood until the Sherrif of Carmarthen drove them out.

The firm stony ridge is followed to Tair Carn Isaf before the steep south-westerly descent leads to a metalled lane (675157) which can be utilised for further descent to Glanaman or Ammanford.

Wherever you stay in the Aman Valley there is the unique atmosphere of the industrial south which compliments the previous rural charms. This is another piece in the Welsh cultural tapestry.

A stronghold controlling the western approach to Llandovery – Carreg-Cennen Castle with the Tair Carn Uchaf/Isaf ridge beyond

Bronze age cairns at the summit of Tair Carn Uchaf

Looking west along the Gower coastline from the Pennard cliffs

CHAPTER 11

DOWN TO THE GOWER COAST
THE AMAN VALLEY TO THREE CLIFFS BAY

This last section will be remembered for its beautiful coastal scenery but its other attributes, if unspectacular, display the surprising diversity of the surrounding countryside.

On climbing out of the busy Aman Valley a very different world is entered – that of the quiet expansive Lliw Hills (not named by the map-makers). These high moors allow the first intimate views of the Gower, thus strengthening further the resolve to press on aided by superb paths on smooth terrain.

Between Lliw and Gower is a relatively uninteresting expanse of semi-rural scenery where the route follows a complex network of paths through field and forest. However, there are some lovely peaceful corners. The Cwm-llwyd oakwoods near Dunvant are a perfect example of nature thriving and deliciously decorating an area so close to less salubrious urban developments.

The lack of steep hills allows a very fast pace to be set through the suburbs west of Swansea, and Bishopston, the gateway to the Gower, is soon reached. From here a most pleasant sylvan limestone valley twists towards the beach by the impressive promontory of Pwlldu Head where the magnificent cliff-top finale commences.

Garnant
The bare hills of Lliw that tower above Glanaman are the last true range that bar the way to the Gower Coast. A lane (670135) leading from the A474 starts the ascent through the picturesque cwm of the Nant Garenig. On its termination a farm track is followed south-eastwards to reach the open fellsides at Banc Cwm-helen, where the windswept grasses of Lliw seem to stretch as far as the eye can see. A south-westerly course then descends to the farm of Henrhyd whose drive is used to reach a lane to the east of Penlle'r-castell, the earthwork remains of an ancient fort (not very impressive).

Mynydd y Gwair and the Upper Lliw Reservoir
Opposite Henrhyd's drive the path continues south-south-west across the golden grassy moors of Mynydd y Gwair giving views of the verdant Clydach Vale

The industrial town of Port Talbot seen from the slopes of Mynydd Garn-fach

which contrasts so strikingly with the stark hills. A high unfenced lane is crossed (667080) before descending slopes (no path marked) towards the Upper Lliw Reservoir. This small lake lies in a wild landscape only slightly tamed by the small spruce plantation on its eastern shores. A distinct rutted track to its north is followed to the west, descending briefly to cross the infant Lliw stream before rising boldly up the slopes of Mynydd Garn-fach.

Mynydd Garn-fach
From the cairned top and across the Lliw moorland the southern scenes are punctuated by cooling towers and scores of smoke-plumed chimneys in the industrial expanses that surround the Neath and Tawe rivers. Beyond them on the eastern side of Swansea Bay lies the giant complex of the Margam Steelworks whose future has for years been precari-

Looking north-east to The Black Mountain massif from the Lliw Hills near Banc Cwm – Garreg-lwyd and Bannau Sir Gaer are the principal tops on the right of the picture

ously balanced in the fickle hands of Whitehall administrators. Further west the marshes of the North Gower and the pastures west of Llanelli are divided by the Loughor estuary.

From Garn-fach's summit a south-westerly descent is made to reach a high unfenced lane (638053) at the eastern end of Cwm Dulais, where a narrow tract of farmland at the valley floor bisects the wild moors.

Felindre and the Penllergaer Forest
The lane is followed south over the bare grassy hill of Pysgodlyn from where it descends to Felindre, a small, quiet village hidden in the depths of the now verdant Lliw Valley. A left turn is made by the church and the following lane

The Upper Lliw Reservoir

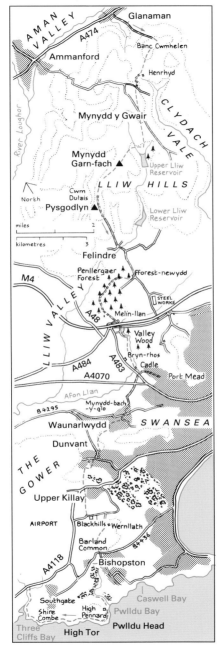

erect stiles, and as a result their fences are regularly pulled down. However an entry can be made at 625994 on the opposite side of the valley via Forestry Commission land. A well trodden path crosses the river via a small bridge and descends to the opposite banks crossing a drainage leat. It then climbs to a well-defined path which winds southwards through the shrubs and trees that line the steep valley sides. A giant copper beech captures the eye for it towers above its neighbours and its colour contrasts pleasingly with their varied green hues. Two ruined, stone-built lodges are passed, and the woodland floor is covered with profuse beds of bluebells and scattered with primroses, a colourful spectacle in spring. An area of reed-covered marshland marked on some maps as a lake is circumvented to the east of Bryn-rhos before the route passes over a small stone bridge, Pont Cadle (624972) at the exit from the woods.

Cadle and Waunarlwydd

Thus far the sprawling suburbs of Swansea and its northern satellites have been avoided but for a three mile section between Cadle and Waunarlwydd there is no escape. This is not hiking country and you will probably feel quite out of place and, rest assured, to the local population you will *look* out of place.

A track from Pont Cadle leads south-eastwards towards the edge of a housing estate. Here a right turn along a minor road then approaches the busy A483 which must be crossed to reach a lane which then crosses the equally busy A4070. The ambience deteriorates further as it passes through an industrial estate, Mynydd-bach-y-glo, and the road continues to the B4295 east of Waunarlwydd (pronounced Wine-ar-loo-with). A right turn along the road is then made and a left at Waunarlwydd

climbs steeply to a junction (638026) where the right fork taken leads southwards lined by pleasant tall hedgerow. The lane is, in turn, left at Fforest-newydd farm where a Forestry Commission access road is used to the edge of the Penllergaer Plantation. The next part of the route is not marked on the OS maps and was kindly shown to me by the chief forester, Bob Price.

After going through the boundary gate a left turn is made following closely the path by the plantation's perimeter until 636013 (where the perimeter veers left) a forestry track leads north-westwards amongst larch and spruce. At 632015 it meets the forestry road which *is* marked on the OS maps. This curves

round steadily from its original westbound direcon to assume a south-easterly one. It crosses a railway cutting and descends to Melin-llan, a cottage by a small bridge spanning the Afon Llan, just a stream at this point. The forest is left on an approach road leading westwards to an M4 roundabout which is crossed to reach the A48.

Valley Wood

The haven south of the M4, in the vale of the Afon Llan and on the northern outskirts of Swansea, is known as Valley Wood. Its main entry on the northern side has been obscured by the recently constructed offices of the Lliw Valley Council who remain oblivious to the needs of public recreation, refusing to

In the Cwm Llwyn woods one of many delightful spots in the western suburbs of Swansea

The chimney in the meadow south of Valley Wood

woodlands (598947), a delightful sanctuary from the city that has spread on all sides. The woods are most beautiful during the early part of summer when many butterflies can be seen hovering on the varied species of wild flower that flourish beneath the twisted sessile oaks, lime and holly.

As the woods are left behind the track widens and a tall red-bricked chimney situated alone in a meadow (597942) is passed. Retrospective views to the north across the plains of Gorseinon include Valley Wood and Penllergaer Forest, and the pale hills of Lliw form the horizon.

Dunvant and Upper Killay
A stony track now leads southwards to emerge at the B4296 between Dunvant and Killay (596937) where a right (west) turn is made on the road which descends and passes over the course of a disused railway. After taking the second road on the left (the cul-de-sac–Fairwood Road) there is a path at its termination which crosses the Clyne River and passes through a small copse before reaching the A4118 at Upper Killay. We can now consider ourselves to have entered the Gower Peninsular and left Swansea behind.

On the opposite side of the road a lane runs southwards past a children's playground towards some houses. A gate by the end house marks the start of the path which makes a south-westerly course over a field before traversing rugby pitches towards the club pavilion. After passing through the car-park it continues south by two more playing pitches and enters deciduous woods via a kissing gate. A left turn (south-east) is then made on a well-defined path that can be muddy after periods of heavy rain. A turning to the right (south-west) is then followed on a less obvious course which begins opposite a very large

Road (610953), thence through a modern housing estate via Caer-Gynydd Road (left), Westwinds Close (right), and then at 604952 the urban sprawl is escaped for a period by a path (marked on OS maps with broken black line) which leads southwards across fields until it meets a well-defined east-west footpath beyond some hedgerow at the foot of the unnamed hill. This is followed westwards passing an ivy-covered, stone chimney which is an air shaft for one of the numerous disused old coal mines in the area. Just after this landmark a narrow path on the left leaves the more obvious track and rises through thick bracken before turning south through mixed rhododendron bush and crosses a tiny stream before leaving woods and going through a campsite.

Blackhills

South of the campsite a minor road is reached (577914) and this is followed eastwards for 600yds to the Blackhills Restaurant. The stile behind the restaurant's car-park (which incidentally took me all of three years to get the council to renew) marks the entry to a series of obscure farmland paths. A southerly course is taken across a field to an opening identified by its adjacent holly bush. Two more small fields are traversed before the path veers eastwards to follow a hedge on the left of the next field. A right turn after going through the second gate in this hedge brings you to a stony farm lane which is followed south-westwards passing a modern farmhouse before reaching some derelict old stone buildings. A further right turn leads past some curiously situated old railway freight wagons which are used as stables. The path continues through an avenue of trees at the northern edge of denser woodland where a streamlet is forded. It then assumes a south-westerly direction across three fields and to the brow of a hill in the fourth (recognised by its telegraph poles). A southerly course from here will lead to a stile preceding a tiny stone bridge over a small tree lined stream (579899). From here the path leads onto Barland Common where on

On the approach to the Bishopston Valley

The narrow wooded section of the Bishopston Valley

occasions I have seen adders. It would therefore be a good idea to don your boots at this point. Outside the summer months the path is quite a good one but it can get overgrown by the thickets of bracken and bramble. In time I hope the increase in use will forge a better passage. Beyond the scrub a small track leads past a small car-park to reach the B4436 to the east of the Kittle Limestone Quarries.

The Bishopston Valley

In the beautiful sylvan valley of Bishopston, owned by the National Trust, walkers can once again feel in their natural element, for this is one of Gower's finest treasures.

From the B4436 a narrow village road leads to Bishopston's square where there are two fine public houses. The Joiner's Arms (my personal favourite) and the larger Valley Hotel would both make excellent choices for a well deserved respite, for they serve good bar meals.

We are now just four and a half miles from the walk's finish at Three Cliffs Bay and many will find this section the

Pwlldu Bay and Pwlldu Head – the path climbs to the headland from the end of the Bishopston Valley on the right.

An easterly view along the Gower coastline from Shire Head

most pleasurable, since that delectable descent from Carmarthen Fan to the Tawe Valley. A signposted footpath leads from the square westwards down to the valley of the Bishopston stream, which, being on a bed of porous limestone, is subterranean at this point except during periods of heavy rain (see alternative route). The path follows the dry bed southwards along meadowland south of Widegate and turns again, this time south-eastwards. The valley sides become steeper and the narrow path hugs the stream's banks, threading through woodland thick with ivy. Suddenly the valley widens and the sky is seen beyond its sides. We are approaching the southern coast at last and it is like a light at the end of a tunnel!

Alternative Descent to Bishopston Valley
After periods of heavy rainfall when the stream bed is no longer dry the approach route to the Bishopston Valley differs. A track from the south-west corner of the village square leads into a field whose eastern hedge is followed to the boundary with the next field. Here a south-south-west course leads to a dingle where a path descends steeply to the Bishopston stream.

Pennard Cliffs
Our route emerges from the valley at Pwlldu Bay. A cottage by a small bridge over the Bishopston stream is passed on a path which rises steeply towards Pwlldu Head. A short climb reveals a huge storm beach of limestone pebbles stretching across the bay and damming the stream. On further ascent, views eastwards along the coastline to the resort of Mumbles can be seen beyond the pastures that crown the limestone cliffs. To the south on a clear day the huge cliffs of Exmoor and the North Devon Coast can clearly be spied across the Bristol Channel.

Three Cliffs Bay (above) and a view along the Pennard Cliffs to the distant sunlit cliffs of Three Cliffs Bay (right)

At the top of the headland from the farm of High Pennard a path traverses fields on a southerly course to the promontory's edge. It then descends to a bracken-cloaked shelf still high above the shoreline and where a narrow path climbs once more to top the pale cliffs.

The path then descends to Deep Slade, a depression that briefly interrupts the magnificent limestone scenery, and, after ascending to the Southgate Lane west of Hunt's Farm, the high clifftop path is resumed. The strata that form this next group are folded so that they are inclined upwards at 45° from the sea shore. Mitchin Hole, situated in High Tor, is Gower's largest coastal cave. Following extensive excavations the bones of elephants, rhinoceros, hyena and humans have been discovered here.

Southgate is a small village which has been much enlarged in modern times to meet the commercial demands of this popular area, but its shops and hotel offer much needed refreshment – a notable feature on a hot day being the general store's large selection of ice-creams. Beyond the village is the delightful little cove, Pobbles Bay, where wide sandy beaches stretch to Oxwich three miles to the west. Jutting out in this expanse are the famous conical bluffs of Three Cliffs Bay and in the view further west rising from the fields of Penmaen is the whaleback sandstone escarpment of Cefn Bryn which is to Gower what the Pennines are to England.

Three Cliffs Bay

Our entry to Three Cliffs Bay from Pobbles is over sandy terrain and skirts the Southgate Golf Links. This sheltered inlet is the estuary of Penard Pill, a narrow stream which meanders on the flat green floor of the valley which twists amongst the woodlands of Parkmill. When the tide is out the best course would be to walk on the beach under the arch in the Three Cliffs, otherwise a

Pennard Castle and the estuary of Pennard Pill

track on the western edge of Pennard Burrows is used.

On the other side of the Pill at Penmaen is a superbly situated campsite which has wonderful views of the bay. For those who want to savour this hard-won beauty spot it would make a very fitting finale, but for others who want to press on the way is along the east side of the estuary, passing the ruins of Pennard Castle and its neighbouring ruined church.

In a final woodland approach to Parkmill a sharp descent is made to the Pill which is crossed at 545892 before reaching the A4118, where there is a convenient cafe.

It will hardly seem like a fortnight and two hundred miles since Llanfair-fechan was left behind. The route has passed through some of the very best Wales has to offer, from the beautifully sculptured mountains of Snowdonia and lonely rolling moors of the Elenydd to the huge dams at Elan and Brianne. The mountains and their perennial elements will almost certainly have tested the spirit and resolve, but those who completed the journey over the Carmarthen Fan and through the suburbs of Swansea to this final section above the Gower cliffs will go home far richer for the experience of the Welsh Coast to Coast Walk.

APPENDIX I

WALES – A HISTORY

After Rome's Retreat

After nearly four hundred years of occupation the Romans were forced by the decline of their Empire to retire from Britain. The Celtic tribesmen were left to regroup and defend themselves against the waves of invaders that were to follow. In Wales they successfully repelled the Picts and Scots but in England they were defeated by the Saxons. This isolated Wales and from this time England and Wales developed, in terms of culture, as two nations.

In the seventh century the Anglo-Saxons made attempts to raid the Welsh. Edwin of Northumbria made the first foray, but the Welsh chief Cadwallon and his allies of Mercia repelled him. King Offa of Mercia then attacked Wales himself. After many years of fighting Offa's Dyke was constructed to mark the boundary between the two neighbours. Both sides respected the borders.

The ninth century brought the onslaught by the Viking marauders who regulaly plundered the Welsh Coast. Rhodri Mawr led the Welsh against them and resisted their raids, which became more sporadic and less intensive until they eventually ended two centuries later.

Rhodri Mawr became the first leader of all Wales. His grandson Hywel Dda (Hywel the Good), a Welsh Chief himself, became famous for his codification of the law. These laws were recognised throughout Wales until the reign of Henry VIII, though after Hywel's death in 949 the country generally returned to disunity and tribalism.

The Norman Conquest of Wales

The harmony that had existed between England under Alfred the Great and Wales under Hywel Dda was not to continue after the defeat of England by William of Normandy at Hastings in 1066. William decided that an independent Wales was not to be tolerated and embarked on what was to become a titanic and protracted struggle.

His soldiers were better armed than those of the Welsh and they made steady, if slow, advances into Welsh territories. Three Norman barons, who became the first in a long line of powerful and troublesome Marcher Lords, made the initial attacks. They were William FitzOsbern, Earl of Hereford, in the South; Roger of Montgomery in Central Wales and Hugh of Avranches who led the attack of North Wales.

Although stiff resistance was offered throughout the next century, the Cambrian Princes were gradually forced to retreat to the hills. When the Normans established themselves in an area they built small 'motte and bailey' castles to garrison their troups. These wooden castles on raised ground were later replaced by more permanent stone fortresses. Around these the first Welsh towns and villages developed, where previously habitation had been scattered.

On the death of Henry I, who had

Llewellyn the Great

been a notorious scourge of Wales, there was a period of disputed accession, and England's temporary weakness was exploited by a new Celtic hero, Owen Gwynedd, who extended his territories virtually to the walls of Chester. In the South lands were recaptured, although not on such a grand scale. The Norman stronghold centred on Pembrokeshire and the Gower was impenetrable.

Henry II took power over England but after an abortive attempt at an invasion via the Berwyn Mountains, he adopted an uneasy truce wtih Owen Gwynedd and his southern conterpart Rhys-ap-Gruffydd.

It is about this time that Rhys-ap-Gruffydd confirmed the grant for the construction of Strata Florida, the Cistertian monastery that was to become such a civilising influence on Central Wales. Rhys is also renowned for congregating the bards for the first 'Eisteddfod' at Cardigan in 1177.

The Warrior Princes

The beginning of the thirteenth century

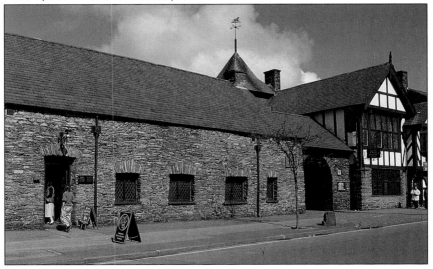
Owain Glyndwr's Parliament House in Machynlleth

saw the rise to power of a new leader, Llewelyn, Prince of Gwynedd, later to become Llewelyn the Great. He noted that the tribalistic structure of the Welsh was inferior to the feudal system adopted by the English, which he was able to institute in his subsequent uniting of Wales, despite some opposition.

Richard I was a contemporary of Llewelyn and his preoccupation with the Holy Wars, combined with his brother John's problems with his barons, meant that the Welsh leader's quest for power proceeded without English hindrance. Llewelyn even married John's daughter Joan, thus attaining some degree of alliance.

The Magna Carta signed by King John promised to give back to Wales the territory that had been taken, and when John died his successor Henry III reluctantly recognised Llewelyn's power over all Wales. Llewelyn died in 1240, and after a brief reign by his son Dafydd, his grandson Llewelyn-ap-Gruffydd proclaimed himself 'Prince of Wales', a title that Henry II acknowledged in the Treaty of Montgomery.

In 1272 Edward I became King of England. He was not tolerant of this independent land on his western borders. For his part, Llewelyn had become overconfident of his powers, for he had long since ceased to pay homage to the English crown, as he was bound to do by agreement. He had also agreed to marry Eleanor, daughter of the traitorous Simon de Montfort, who had led the rebellion that had captured and briefly imprisoned Henry III. Diplomatic relations deteriorated.

In 1277 Edward attacked and by the summer of that year all Wales, except Gwynedd and Anglesey from where Llewelyn ruled, was in English hands. When Edward sailed his fleet through the Menai Straits, thereby dividing the two remaining strongholds, Llewelyn was forced to accept defeat. In the treaty that followed, he forfeited his powers over South and Central Wales; his marriage to Eleanor de Montfort was forbidden, and he was again compelled to pay homage to the English throne.

Llewelyn's brother Dafydd broke the treaty when, in 1282, he attacked and captured Howarden. This inspired an uprising and Llewelyn was forced into the fray. Edward repeated the tactics of the previous encounter and again penned the rebels within Gwynedd. Llewelyn, with a small guard, slipped through the English line and endeavoured to gain support from the South. This initiative came to an abrupt end on the outskirts of Builth Wells however, where Llewelyn was killed by an English knight. Dafydd was executed and Wales yet again lost its independence.

Edward built a series of powerful castles including Conwy, Harlech, Caernarfon and Beaumaris, all still standing proudly today. They must have presented an image of irresistible domination to the Welshmen of those times.

Following this subjugation the next few generations of Welsh warriors fought with the English in the battlefields of France. It is said that leeks, for so long the symbol of Welsh National Pride, were picked and worn as trophies by the victorious Gwent Bowmen from the fields of Crecy.

A New Prince

Owain Glyndwr (Owen Glendower) was a respected citizen who had a place at the English Court, and it came as a great surprise when, after a meeting with rebels at Glyndyfrdwy in 1400, he was declared Prince of Wales. Henry IV sent an army to quell the rebellion but, after a year of harsh anti-Welsh laws, the war escalated and Conwy was recaptured for Wales by the Tudors, a family who later in the century were to emerge as rulers of England. Glyndwr was victorious at Nant Hyddgant to the north of Pumlumon (Plynlymon) (see Chapter 6). He then took Aberystwyth and Harlech after defeating the powerful Marcher Lord, Edmund Mortimer. In

Henry Tudor who after the Battle of Bosworth took the English throne as Henry VII

1404 Glyndwr, who was by now in control of most of Wales, set up a Welsh Parliament at Machynlleth and had himself 'officially' crowned 'Prince of Wales'.

In 1407, as the rebellion lost some impetus, Harlech was lost to the English under Henry V. By 1410 all was lost and Glyndwr withdrew into obscurity.

The aftermath of this last Welsh uprising was devastating. Severe laws were introduced barring Welsh citizens from congregating in any numbers without prior permission. They were not allowed to hold municiple office. The lands of Glyndwr's rebels were seized by the crown, while others were forced to retreat from the incessantly looted towns and villages and attempted to forge new lives on the less hospitable moorlands.

The Tudors

In the thirty years that followed the battle of St Albans in 1455, England was divided by the Wars of the Roses, in which the Houses of Lancaster and York disputed the accession to the throne. The Yorkists led by Edward IV gained power in 1461, and of great significance to Wales in the following period were Edward's successful efforts to reduce the powers of the Marcher Barons, who had been particularly perfidious in their allegiances.

It might seem inconceivable that after centuries of oppression a Welshman would rule all England, but such a man, Henry Tudor, a direct descendant of Llewelyn the Great, had become leader of the House of Lancaster, being the grandson of John of Gaunt. His forced exile to Brittany ended when he landed at Milford Haven and marched northward to Machynlleth gathering an army of Welshmen. He confronted the Yorkist troups of Richard III at Bosworth Field, near Leicester. Victory was Henry's, and thus in the year of 1485 a Welshman was crowned King of England.

The Battle at Bosworth effectively ended the Wars of the Roses and Henry secured the peace by marrying a Yorkist, Elizabeth, daughter of Edward IV. The restrictions imposed on the Welsh by Henry IV were lifted, and ambitious Welshmen soon began to move into England. In an early reform, Henry set up the Council of Wales, based at Ludlow. This precursor of the present Welsh Office was an administrative body set up to carry out Privy Council orders and supervise the judicial system within the principality.

In 1509 Henry VIII succeeded his father to the throne. His acts of 1536 and 1543 officially united England and Wales. The Welsh Laws of Hywel the Good were replaced by English Law, although Wales was allowed to retain its own law courts. Exchequers were established at Carmarthen, Denbigh, and Brecon alongside the already functioning one at Caernarfon. Because of its proximity to England, Monmouth was attached to the Courts of Westminster. This, and the fact that the county received the slightly preferential treatment afforded to England, had the effect of gradually alienating Monmouthshire from the rest of the principality.

The language used in the law courts was English, and this led to the eventual decline in the use of the Welsh language, especially in the urban areas of the South. As a result English became the language of the gentry and the scholars, who played down their Welsh origins. They were asked, about this period, to adopt surnames, as the English had done, for reasons of identification. The Welsh way of adding the father's name was found unsatisfactory and so, for example, a man known as Twm ap Hywel (Tom, son of Hywel) would probably have been Anglicized to Tom Powell.

The Act of 1536 required each Welsh county to be represented in Parliament by a knight of the shire, and each shire town, with the exception of poverty stricken Harlech, had a burgess as its representative. The Marcher Lordships were abolished and replaced by the new counties of Denbigh, Montgomery, Radnor and Brecknock.

There was little Welsh resistance to

the Reformation and even to the suppression of the monasteries, which had long ceased to contribute greatly to the local communities. Indeed, there were many cases of monks being prosecuted for criminal activities. Abbot Salisbury of Valle Crucis (Llangollen), for instance, was convicted of highway robbery, and a monk from Strata Florida was jailed for counterfeiting. This did little to endear the religious orders to the people. The lands held by the monasteries and

the Roman Catholic Church were confiscated and sold to laymen, usually members of the local gentry.

In 1563 Elizabeth I commissioned Richard Davies, Bishop of St Davids, to translate from Latin to Welsh both the Bible and a book of prayer. He collaborated with a notable scholar, William Salesbury, to complete the works without the Old Testament. Twenty years later William Morgan published a complete Bible translation. It has been said

that these works helped to preserve the real Welsh language and to prevent its degradation into dialects and eventual decline, as the people heard good Welsh spoken every time they attended church.

Although Wales was involved in the Civil War the effects on the principality were few, and most of the battles were over the border in England. Largely its people were supporters of the crown because of previous allegiances to the Tudors.

The Winds of Change

Until the end of the sixteenth century the principality had been almost entirely pastoral. Now there was increased activity in the exploitation of minerals. Lead was found in abundance in Cardiganshire and the mines brought prosperity for the area. The large demand for timber as a fuel and to make ships rapidly diminished the Welsh forests, and the need for coal as an alternative fuel became evident. Coal was mined at this time in the coastal areas of Glamorgan, Carmarthenshire, Pembrokeshire and Flintshire and much of it was exported to Ireland and France. The seeds of industrialisation were sown.

The Establishment of Presbyterianism

By the eighteenth century the established church had become remote from the problems of the average Welshman. The Bishops elected were entirely English, many of them totally uninterested in their sees, and thus it was that Welsh Presbyterianism began to take root. At first the pioneers of Methodism remained within the framework of the orthodox church, but in 1811 the break did come, with eight Calvinist Methodists being ordained at Bala and thirteen at Llandeilo. The movement's success, which was largely due to the fiery enthusiasm of early pioneers, is very evident, for within the Welsh towns and villages their austere chapels outnumber the traditional parish churches.

Industrial Revolution

The industrial revolution came a little later to Wales than to England. The mountains of Glamorgan and West Monmouthshire were rich in coal, iron ore and limestone, which made them ideal centres for iron making. In 1759 the Dowlais Iron Works in Merthyr Tydfil, which was to become the largest in the world, was established, soon to be followed by others at Ebbw Vale, Tredegar and Blaenafon.

The building of the railways proved to be the catalyst in the growth of the South Wales coalfields, and peaceful valleys became scarred with the black tips and winding gear of the pits, towering above the lines of terraced miners' cottages. These mines attracted Welshmen from the rural areas, which were starved of employment, initiating a shift in the population to urban communities.

In North Wales, slate-quarrying had become a major industry. The grey terraced towns of Llanberis, Blaenau Ffestiniog and Bethesda grew as their mountains were reduced and disfigured by the ravages of an industry that was as tough on its workers as on the landscape. Death and serious injury were commonplace within these communities.

Decline and Revolt

After an economic boom during the Napoleonic Wars, the nineteenth century held much tribulation for Wales. Its industries went into decline and those who held a job were grossly underpaid, overtaxed and exploited. It was in this climate that the violent Chartist riots of the eighteen thirties took place. The worst conflict occurred at Merthyr Tydfil, where twenty seven were killed and seventy were injured, including twenty soldiers.

There was also trouble in rural areas where local communities rebelled against the owners of the turnpike roads who demanded a toll for passage. The tollgates on these roads were the targets of the Rebecca Rioters. They had become a symbol of oppression to the impoverished hill farmers and tinkers. The name Rebecca came from the book of Genesis which said, 'And they blessed Rebekah

Rebecca leading the toll gate rioters, 1839

and said unto her, thou art our sister, be thou the mother of thousands of millions and let thy seed possess the gate of those which hate them.' The rioters, dressed in female attire, destroyed the gates. Such was the degree of popular support for the Rebeccas that little information as to their identity was offered to the authorities.

In the second half of the century there was much activity by the newly formed trade unions who fought vehemently for workers' rights and wages in a period of strife that lasted to the turn of the twentieth century. Although there were suc-

cesses, their militancy was sometimes their undoing, as in the Slate Miners' Strike of 1900-1903 where the workmen, spurred on by a previous victory, were forced to capitulate and return with no gains. The resulting lack in continuity of supplies had led to a search for alternative materials for the manufacture of tiles, and between 1898 and 1914 the workforce was halved.

Unfortunately there has been further exploitation of the Welsh countryside for new water schemes. The flooding of the Tryweryn Valley near Bala for Llyn Celyn resulted in the loss of a village and was received with massive protest, but to this day similar ventures are undertaken with little thought for the inhabitants.

Through the World Wars

The First World War brought about a great expansion in Welsh Industry. The government assisted the companies to increase productivity to meet the higher demands of wartime. By the conclusion of the war the coal mines of Belgium and France had been destroyed, thereby creating higher demand for Welsh coal. The period of prosperity lasted until 1923, when Wales sank into a depression which had afflicted much of the western world. This depression was to last longer in Wales than in other countries – until the Second World War, when it was made a development area, offering firms who moved there grants and incentives. Thus new industries were introduced to diversify the economy, which had previously failed so badly. Industrial estates such as the one at Fforest Fach, north of Swansea, were built, and gradually light industry has replaced the likes of coal and steel which decline to this day under the threat of cheap imports. The Forestry Commission, set up to remedy the lack of wood supplies following the First World War, was responsible for planting vast conifer forests not only in the rural areas but also in the redundant 'pit valleys'.

In 1963 the Welsh Language Society was founded. Its objective was the equality of the Welsh and English Languages. They turned their attentions to the English road signs which they demanded should be bi-lingual, and in this they were successful, although their methods, such as the destruction of offending signs, were dubious.

Plaid Cymru, the Welsh Nationalist Party, won its first seat in 1966 and became a real threat to Labour's dominance in the seventies, though their influence now seems to be receding. Their aim for a 'Free Wales' seems unlikely and not universally supported amongst Welshmen, but they illustrate the fierce nationalism that has re-emerged and maybe in such a climate the cultures and idiosyncrasies of this nation will survive the eroding influences of time.

APPENDIX II

FORESTRY

The Cambrian Forests
The growth of forestry as an industry coincided with the decline of those of coal, lead and slate mining, although, in employment terms, it did not fully compensate for the losses. In 1919 when the Forestry Commission was founded, Britain's woodland cover had shrunk to around 5%, which meant that it had to import a large quantity of timber to cope with the increasing demands of industry (pit props for the coal industry; fenceposts; pulp for the paper-makers, and material for the building industry). To increase the crop quickly the Commission decided to import fast-growing conifers and group them in vast plantations on land which was unsuitable for profitable farming.

Unfortunately, in their zeal for expansion of the forests, planners have shown little care for protecting the beauty or equilibrium of the countryside. A glance at the map reveals that Wales, especially in its central regions, has become very densely afforested. Few would argue with the siting of plantations on the barren lower Elenydd marshlands (the northern reaches of the Tywi Forest), but the Dyfi Forest has now almost obscured the beautiful Tarren Hills, north of Machynlleth; likewise the Ystwyth and Hafren Forests have distorted the area to the south and west of Pumlumon and robbed it of its character. These are just two of many examples which have antagonised both walkers and conservationists alike.

In its bid to woo the affections of the public at large the Commission has strategically placed roadside picnic sites and has waymarked short walks through the forests. Its wide flinted roads even offer walkers quick access to some of the more remote mountains and moors, but often at the expense of true rights of way which have been overplanted and forgotten.

The Mechanics of Modern Forestry
In modern forests seeds are grown in controlled nurseries for two or three years before the saplings are permanently planted in stands of up to a thousand per acre. After twenty years they have grown to a height of about twenty feet, and at this stage the poorer trees are felled to give the others more room to grow. This thinning-out process is repeated every four or five years. The timber is used for fencing and wood pulp. It takes between fifty and sixty years (depending on type and conditions) for the trees to mature, by which time they will have reached a height of a hundred feet or more. The mature trees are then felled and the site is cleared in order to make way for further plantations, and the process begins once more. Successful foresters will always have sections of their plantations at different stages of development, enabling a team of men to be permanently employed on the various tasks, thus aiding the stability of labour.

By far the most successful tree in the Welsh forests has been the Sitka Spruce, an import from Western America. It has flourished in high exposed sites including those with thin acid or peaty soils, and matures quickly to a hundred-foot giant timber producer. The Norway Spruce, better known as the common Christmas Tree, is a native of Northern Europe, and is distinguished from the Sitka by its more yellow-green foliage and longer cones. It is however more susceptible to frosts.

Two types of larch and a non-evergreen conifer are widely planted. Older forests such as the Coed-y-Brenin, Dyfi and Ystwyth contain many European Larch trees, a species which has not been as successful in Wales as in more northern latitudes. Its cousin the Japanese Larch is faster growing and has a much greater resistance to fungal attack and is now therefore widely used. In summer the broader Japanese Larch can be recognised by its more bluish needles, and in winter its branches have a reddish hue.

The Scots Pine is the only conifer native to the British Isles. It is not a good timber producer however, suffering badly on exposed sites. Far superior is the Lodgepole Pine, a fast growing species which can be planted in poor soils. Its appearance is similar to the Scots Pine but it has a lighter green foliage. A third species, the Corsican Pine, has a blackish bark and has grown well on the sandy soils by the Harlech Coast.

Other common species in the Welsh Forests are the giant Douglas Fir imported from the American 'Rockies', and Western Hemlock, easily recognised by its bright green, fern-like foliage. Both grow well on the lower slopes and valleys.

The Future
At the time of writing the future of the Forestry Commission is in doubt for it is believed that it will be removed from State ownership. Privately owned forests are already increasing rapidly and account for 80% of all new plantations. Before 1988 huge tax benefits and grants from the public purse led to large-scale investment in this sector of the market by forest groups acting on behalf of individuals looking for tax dodges.* The production of wood was of secondary importance, as to avoid tax payable from the proceeds of the crop the investors would sell their forests (without the burden of Capital Gains Tax) before they reached maturity (ten years is said to be the ideal ownership period). The Commission also offered free advice and help to set up these new ventures started.

If privatisation of the Commission does go ahead I hope that provision will be made to retain access through the forests, for it seems that no legal right of way exists except on the public footpaths, few of which still exist in reality. It would also be necessary for the Secretary of State for Wales to ensure that no new forests be planted in ecologically sensitive areas or those of great beauty, because the privately owned companies would almost certainly be less image-conscious and less accountable to the general public. It would also be better if incentives were offered for planting the less profitable but more ecologically satisfactory slow-growing, broad-leafed woodlands, whose numbers were reduced drastically by the freak storms of October 1987.

(*Benefits largely withdrawn in the 1988 Budget.)

APPENDIX III

ACCOMMODATION

Although the walk is divided into eleven stages based on valley camping, hotels or hostels, it may be suitable to adjust this according to personal taste. Mountain campers will usually wish to stop in some romantic high mountain location, particularly in fine weather, whereas others may wish to split some of the longer days and stay at obvious intermediate points. I have therefore listed accommodation available at the end of each of the described stages, plus additional accommodation and campsites at intermediate stages and other useful places off route (that would involve some change of plan) to allow the traveller to plan an itinerary with the maximum flexibility. When planning use of this accommodation it is worth remembering that many of the Youth Hostels and Hotels close for periods during the winter months and it is essential to check on their availability at an early stage.

In almost all cases the mountain and main routes are of similar distance – the total length of the main route being 213 miles and the mountain route 220 miles – the main difference between the two being in height differential.

1   ACROSS THE CARNEDDAU   Llanfairfechan to Helyg   15 miles

The Myrtle Wood Hotel   ☎ Llanfairfechan/0248 680735
Helyg (Climbers' Club Hut at 692602 available for booking by BMC members)
Gwern-y-gof Isaf (campsite and self-catering bunkhouse)   ☎ Capel Curig/06904 276
Gwern gof Uchaf (campsite 1 mile west of Gwern-y-gof Isaf)
Off-route accommodation:
Roewen Youth Hostel (3 miles east of the northern end of the route at 747721 bookable through Colwyn Bay YHA   ☎ Colwyn Bay/0492 531406)
Idwal Cottage Youth Hostel (2 miles west of Helyg on the A5)   ☎ Bethesda/0248 600225
Cobdens Hotel (☎ Capel Curig/06904 243) and Bryn Tyrch Hotel (☎ Capel Curig/06904 223 or 352) in Capel Curig – 3 miles east of Helyg on the A5

2   THE GLYDERS AND SNOWDON   Helyg to Nantgwynant   13 miles

Bryngwnant Youth Hostel (by Llyn Gwynant at 642513)   ☎ Beddgelert/076686 251
Llys Elen Guest House, Nantgwynant (632511)   ☎ Beddgelert/076686 446
Glan Gwynant Country Guest House, Nantgwynant (639514)   ☎ Beddgelert/076686 440
Lyndi-isaf Farm, Nantgwynant (campsite by Llyn Dinas)
Hafod-y-llan Farm, Nantgwynant (campsite near the Watkin Path, Snowdon)
Hafod-y-rhisgl (campsite by north shore of Llyn Gwynant)
Intermediate accommodation:
Pen-y-Gwryd Hotel   ☎ Llanberis/0286 870211
Pen-y-Pass Youth Hostel   ☎ Llanberis/0286 870420
Off-route accommodation:
Tanronen Hotel (☎ Beddgelert/076686 347) and Prince Llewellyn Hotel (☎ Beddgelert/076686 242) in Beddgelert – 2 miles south-west of Nantgwynant

3   THE MOELWYNS   Nantgwynant to Trawsfynydd   19 miles

White Lion Inn, Trawsfynydd   ☎ Trawsfynydd/076687 277
Cae Pant, Trawsfynydd (campsite)
Intermediate accommodation:
Oakley Arms, Tan-y-Bwlch, Maentwrog   ☎ Maentwrog/076685 277
The Old Rectory, Maentwrog (B & B)   ☎ Maentwrog/076685 202 or 305
Bryntirion Farm, Gellilydan (B & B) (681391)   ☎ Maentwrog/076685 321
Llwyn Farm, Gellilydan, Maentwrog (Camping at 683392)

4   ROUTES THROUGH THE RHINOGS   Trawsfynydd to Barmouth   20 miles

Plas Mynach, Llanaber Road, Barmouth   ☎ Barmouth/0341 280252
Belgrave, Marine Parade, Barmouth   ☎ Barmouth/0341 280369
Aran Hotel, Marine Parade, Barmouth   ☎ Barmouth/0341 280122
Campsite 1 mile north of Barmouth at 606170
Arthog (campsite south of the Mawddach Estuary at 653149)
Intermediate accommodation:
Craig Isaf Farm, Cwm Nantcol (B & B at 635259)
Campsite at 641274 in Cwm Nantcol, Rhinogs
Off-route accommodation:
Cwm Bychan Farm, Rhinogs (campsite at 647315, 1½ miles west of the mountain route)
Kings Youth Hostel, Dolgellau (683161)   ☎ Dolgellau/0341 422392
Bontddu (campsite at 663186 on the north shore of the Mawddach)
Bontddu Hall Hotel, Bontddu   ☎ Bontddu/034149 661
George III Hotel, Penmaenpool   ☎ Penmaenpool/0341422 525

The last four entries would be useful for those who quit the ridge at Llawlech or Diffwys to cross the Mawddach Estuary on the Penmaenpool Toll Bridge.

5   CADAIR IDRIS AND THE TARRENS   Barmouth to Machynlleth   18 miles (25 miles)

Dyfi Forester Hotel, Doll St, Machynlleth   ☎ Machynlleth/0654 2004
Wynnstay Hotel, Maengwyn St, Machynlleth   ☎ Machynlleth/0654 2003
Garth Farm (campsite 1 mile east of Machynlleth at 760016)
Intermediate accommodation:
Gwastadfryn Farm, Llanfihangel (campsite at 677098)
Riverside Cafe, Abergynolwyn (B & B)   ☎ Abergynolwyn/065477 235
Off-route accommodation:
Tynycornel Hotel, Talyllyn (3 miles east of Abergynolwyn)   ☎ Abergynolwyn/065477 288

6   HYDDGEN AND PUMLUMON   Machynlleth to Pant Mawr   17 miles

Glansevern Arms, Pant Mawr   ☎ Llangurig/05515 240
Intermediate accommodation:
Eisteddfa Gurig Farm/Cafe (B & B and campsite)   ☎ Ponterwyd/097085 300
Off-route accommodation:
Dyffryn Castell Inn, Ponterwyd (3 miles west of the route)   ☎ Ponterwyd/097085 237
George Borrow Hotel, Ponterwyd (5 miles west of the route)   ☎ Ponterwyd/097085 230
Blue Bell Inn, Llangurig (3½ miles east of the route)   ☎ Llangurig/05515 254

7   THE GREAT RESERVOIRS   Pant Mawr to Elan Village   19 miles

Elan Valley Hotel, Elan Village   ☎ Rhayader/0597 810448
Off-route accommodation:
Wyeside Caravan Park, Rhayader (campsite 3 miles east of the route)
Lion Royal Hotel, West St, Rhayader   ☎ Rhayader/0597 810202
Elan Hotel, West St, Rhayader   ☎ Rhayader/0597 810373